The Culture of Heaven

and the cultures of earth

James Litsey

DEDICATION

To Lisa, my faithful partner and true friend,

and to all my favorite sons and daughters:
Matt, Rachel, Fatu, Laura, Sinnah, Sento, Jack, and Will.

It must be difficult to live with a crazy man,
and even more difficult to love him.

So thanks.

CONTENTS

ACKNOWLEDGMENTS

Cover art by William P. Litsey

Scripture quotations are from The ESV Bible (The Holy Bible, English Standard Version), copyright 2001 by Crossway. Used by permission. All rights reserved. All italics were added by the author for emphasis.

1
INTRODUCTION: ABIMELECH'S OBSERVATION

These next sentences are hard, but this book is about the possibility they might be true. Maybe Jesus didn't come so that we could live better on earth. Maybe he came to bring us to heaven. Maybe following Jesus won't make our lives here better by earth's measure.

Following Jesus will, however, make our lives on earth different. What we believe, how we think, the way we live, our aspirations, our values, our desires, our motivations, our evaluation of success and failure, *all* that will be different, part of a heavenly way of life, a new culture, different from every culture ever found anywhere on earth.

The purpose of this little book is simply to welcome you to this new culture, the Culture of Heaven. I'm praying reading it helps you as much as writing it helped me.

Here's how it came to be. God has led my family down a peculiar pathway that has involved several different cultures. My wife and I adopted three girls from Sierra Leone after the civil war there. Trust me, there was some culture learning involved in that adventure, on the part of both the girls and the rest of the family!

A few years later, we felt God calling us to live in Africa as missionaries. Part of our pre-departure training was a year in Quebec learning French. Another culture. For three years we lived in a rural part of Guinea, West Africa. More culture learning. After returning home, we began helping resettle refugees in our town, mainly Burmese Christians. Still more culture learning.

We are currently hosting a family of African asylum seekers in our home. Yet another culture. Do you see a pattern? God seems intent on having us interface with culture after culture... So this cultural analysis of Jesus' teachings didn't come about because I'm particularly clever or studious or creative. It's simply because God led me down this pathway, and gave me a viewpoint I wouldn't have otherwise.

Anyone with that background would have started to see Jesus' teachings in terms of culture. As I did so, I came to realize that the new way of living Jesus taught his disciples had many elements of a new culture. He was teaching everybody who would ever follow him a culture that was fundamentally different from every other culture that had ever existed on earth. It was the culture of heaven, and he wanted it to be the culture of his kingdom. Everything started to make more sense to me: Jesus' teachings on following him, his expectations of me, some of the problems of the early church, some of the problems with our churches...

I don't think there is anything new in this little book. These are all old teachings. I doubt this is even a new way of looking at them. But it was new to me, and the concept of a heavenly culture has helped me greatly. Maybe it will help you as well.

Let me explain a few things. First, I wanted to keep this short enough to read in a single session, like maybe one Sunday afternoon. I tend to lose the point of a book if I must read it in pieces over several days. Because this book is short, it will move quickly. You'll find some pretty big points made without a lot of explanation or illustration. I want you to be able to read the whole thing then digest the whole thing. Warning, the first parts are maybe a bit tedious and repetitive. Just push through them. The last parts will be a lot more interesting, but only if you've read the first parts.

Also, there is a lot a scripture here. I confess that when I read a book with scripture references I almost never look them up if they're not right there on the page. That's why I put most of them right there for you. I know these scriptures are very familiar to most of us, but please take the time to actually read them again. I love it when someone shows me a scripture I've read a hundred times, connects it to other scriptures, and makes a concept come alive for me. I hope that happens for you at least once while reading this book.

Finally, there will almost certainly be something in here that will upset you. That's not my aim, but it has been my experience that these topics provoke strong emotions. Write me off if you wish. But don't write off the culture of heaven.

We'll talk more about the culture of heaven in a minute. First, let me ask you a question. How does the world see God's presence in our lives?

In Gen 26, God blessed Isaac so that he became wealthy, actually *very* wealthy. Despite having previously caught Isaac in a big lie, the pagan king Abimelech nonetheless noticed Isaac's great wealth and correctly attributed it to God's blessing. In Gen 26:28 he says "We see plainly that the Lord has been with you."

Bottom line: Abimelech became convinced God was at work in Isaac's life because of Isaac's material wealth. What Abimelech had seen of Isaac's character and behavior didn't impress him. He was impressed by Isaac's riches. It's not just Isaac. We see the blessing = material wealth connection with Abraham, Jacob, Joseph, David, Solomon, etc. It's a pattern.

Old Testament: Blessing is material wealth, and the world is impressed.

Fast forward about 2000 years. Jesus redefines blessing. Who is blessed now? According to Jesus in Luke 6:20-23, it is the poor, hungry, mournful, hated, excluded, reviled, and slandered. People like him, like Jesus.

New Testament: Blessing is not material wealth, and the world is not impressed.

What about us? If it's not wealth, then what *should* make our world conclude that the Lord has been with us? Maybe God intends the evidence of our blessedness be the unearthly things we do and the unearthly way we live.

> "In the same way, let your light shine before others, so that they may see your good works and give glory to your Father who is in heaven."
>
> Matt 5:16

> Now when they saw the boldness of Peter and John, and perceived that they were uneducated, common men, they were astonished. And they recognized that they had been with Jesus.
>
> Acts 4:13

The old manifestation of God's presence in a man's life was material riches. Isaac was a perfect example. The new manifestation of God's presence in a man's life is Holy Spirit-empowered obedience. Jesus is the perfect example.

In this respect, the unredeemed world is the same today as in Isaac's time. It still believes material wealth is the measure of God's blessing. Unfortunately, many in the church believe it too. That's a big problem. Under Jesus' redefinition of blessing, it's simply not true. In fact, Jesus says "But woe to you who are rich, for you have received your consolation." Further, the Bible never tells us to imitate any of the rich men in scripture. Instead we are repeatedly told to imitate Christ, who was not rich.

So why then do we still want to live like Isaac but not live like Christ? It's simple, I think. Isaac died a rich man, and Jesus died on a cross. For the most part, we're not interested in this Jesus-style blessing, because we can see it leads to suffering. We find Isaac-style blessing much more appealing.

Why? Because even we in the church still harbor so much earth culture within us. We let our earth culture tell us what blessing is and how a blessed life looks. We study and work and plan and even sacrifice so that we can live like Isaac. According to earth culture, that's the deal of life. Regardless of whether or not we're in a church, that's pretty much the bargain to which we all agree, whether we admit it or not. But what if that changed?

What if we studied and worked and planned and sacrificed not to live like Isaac, but to live like Jesus? To think like him and act like him and *be* like him? What if we lived the culture of heaven? What if we even *tried* to live the culture of heaven?

What if our churches helped us discover heaven culture? What if our churches demonstrated heaven culture for us, taught it to us, and (yikes!) expected it of us? What if our aspirations and most fundamental assumptions of reality began to reflect the culture of heaven? What if all of us began to believe what Jesus said about blessing? And what if we began to live like we believed it? What if we were OK with all the associated implications for this life? What if we suffered because of God's righteousness? And what if we rejoiced when we were mistreated instead of looking to sue someone? What if the world watched us and ridiculed us and we didn't even care? What if they asked us to explain ourselves and our only response was that we believe Jesus? That we don't just believe *in* Jesus, we believe that everything he said is true.

I'm asking these questions not because I know the answers, but because I want to know. I want to know Christ. I want to live like Jesus. I admit I only "sort of" want it. But at least I'm beginning to *want* to want it. And I want my church, and you and your church, to want it too.

Brothers and sisters, we were made for heaven. Once there, we won't ever live anywhere else. We won't want to. Heaven will be our home forever, our last and best place to live. God wants us to remind ourselves of

7

that continually. We'll live differently here now if we keep remembering we'll be living there forever.

Life in heaven will, of course, be very different from our present life. There will be a new way of living, a new culture. We'll treat each other differently. Better. We'll have a new way of thinking about most everything, new values, new aspirations. Many things that seem important now won't seem important at all then.

There will be another big difference. There is no sin in heaven. None of sin's implications. None of sin's consequences. We can't even imagine a world completely without sin. But actually, we aren't limited by our imagination. Jesus told us a lot about it.

He didn't tell us everything. Just what we need to know now. Mostly, he told us about heaven's culture. Here's why. He wants us, the redeemed, to begin living the culture of heaven now, while we're still on earth. I know it sounds weird and impossible. It sounded weird and impossible to people two thousand years ago too. But that's what he wants. He even said he'd help us do it. That's why the Holy Spirit was sent, to help us live heaven culture now.

> "If you love me, you will keep my commandments. And I will ask the Father, and he will give you another Helper, to be with you forever, even the Spirit of truth, whom the world cannot

receive, because it neither sees him nor knows him. You know him, for he dwells with you and will be in you."

John 14:15-17

There is a problem, though.

If we start living the culture of heaven while we're on earth, we may become enough like Jesus that the world will treat us like it treated him. Actually it may *mis*treat us like it *mis*treated him. That's the catch, remember. We don't want to be mistreated like Jesus was. So I'm ashamed to say we've proposed an alternative to living heaven culture.

"How about this, Jesus? Why don't you just help us live our earth culture better? Here and now. Help us manage our time and money and family and career better than people who don't have you to help them. Help us be healthy, wealthy, and wise. Then we'll be happy. People will like us. They might even admire us, like they did Isaac.

"Help us live our earth culture better than all those unbelievers do, Lord. And when we're in the earth culture winner's circle, we'll be sure to thank you for it. We'll even thank you out loud in public if you want. But living heaven culture? Can't we just save that until we're actually in heaven?"

But Jesus doesn't bargain. He doesn't need to. After all, he is the Lord of the universe. He has already decided what following him means. And he has decided that following him means living heaven culture starting now, right here on earth.

So here's *his* deal. We follow him his way. Or we don't follow him at all. That's the only deal he offers.

"But what about grace?" some of you may be asking. Grace is God's gift to all who try to imitate Jesus, since they will all ultimately fail. Grace frees us to try. I'm pretty sure grace wasn't intended to excuse us from trying.

I hope this book will help you decide to try, to see your life as a sacrifice to him, to walk away from your earth culture, and to allow him to teach you to live the culture of heaven on earth. Like Jesus did. No matter how the world reacts. And to help your church try to live heaven culture too.

It might hurt. Maybe a lot. But remember, it will only hurt until you die. Then the best part of your life will start and never end.

2

WHAT *IS* THE CULTURE OF HEAVEN?

Mom made Dad take her to a symphony concert once in a while. He pretty much hated to go, but he went because he loved Mom. I often heard his wistful country-boy lament, "Your mother is making me go get a dose of culture Saturday night." Dad thought culture had something to do with oboes and violins and neckties. That's *not* what we're talking about.

Simply put, culture is everything we do, think, and value, and why we do it, think it, and value it. Culture includes our worldview, our complex synthesis of seen and unseen reality, what we mean by "the way things are." Every culture on earth is astonishingly complex, even the cultures of technologically "simple" peoples.

Some aspects of culture are easy to see, like the way we dress, what we eat, and how we talk. Some are less easily seen, like what we respect or admire, how we

11

choose friends or spouses, and how we learn. Some are nearly invisible, like our perceptions of individuality, how we perceive truth, etc. Our culture gives us a way to understand what is going on around us. It helps us know where we fit in our social structures. It's like an invisible pathway through life that we share with people like us.

In fact, our culture even defines the phrase "people like us." It isn't too much to say that culture is what makes living in groups possible. Even the most individualistic among us share a culture with other individuals. Our culture gives us templates for social interactions as menial as buying groceries and as complex as raising a child.

Not only does everything we do and think derive from our culture, our culture even tells us what we *ought* to do and how we *ought* to think. Our culture not only defines "normal" life, but also the *best* life, what is honorable or praiseworthy, what sort of life is worth pursuing. Our culture tells us what is right and wrong, polite and rude. Our culture tells us what to applaud and what to correct, as well as how to applaud and how to correct. I hope you're getting the idea. Our culture is everything about us. One might even say that in some sense we *are* our culture and our culture is us.

The cultural complexity of earth is astonishing. Imagine a map of the world, but instead of sharp lines between hundreds of countries, imagine fuzzy lines between thousands of cultures. It would have to be updated continually. Some cultures die "natural" deaths. Sometimes more powerful cultures overwhelm and eventually absorb less powerful cultures. Areas of cultural overlap are continually shifting. New cultures are being born as well.

To make everything even more complicated, individual cultures change over time. For example, cultural standards of politeness and rudeness aren't fixed over time. Even the list of activities subject to being done politely or rudely changes over time. For example politeness and rudeness in a text message is not the same as politeness and rudeness in actual speech, so texting manners have recently been added to my culture. At the same time, the knowledge of household uses of woodland plants, once an important part of my culture, is disappearing.

Each of us identify with a culture. Even if we leave home and live in a far distant place with a very different culture, we still carry our cultural "home" inside us. We will use this "inside" culture to evaluate the culture around us. In such situations, most people will eventually learn to navigate their adopted culture but likely will always identify primarily with their first culture. Few people can truly become equally at home in more than one culture.

Everyone on earth has a culture that in certain ways defines him. It is easy to look around the earth and see that these cultures can differ greatly. But there are common elements. Such characteristics are called "cultural universals." For example, every culture has rituals associated with birth and death. How many cultural universals exist? Different students of culture will give different answers.

Anthropologists love to compile lists of cultural universals. If you do a Google search you'll find several lists of varying lengths, but the most important cultural universal likely won't be on any of these lists. It is sin. Sin is woven into the fabric of every culture on earth. In this one fundamental way, all cultures on earth are alike. They all deal with sin. Here's what I mean:

We know that all humans sin and fall short of the glory of God. We also know that sin tends to erode relationships, pit us against each other, and impede cooperation. Unchecked sin would make living together impossible. Human society could not exist without some mechanism of "managing" or at least regulating the effects of sin. We could look at each culture on earth as one of many systems by which sinful people have learned to live together. For example, every society needs an orderly way to assign husbands to wives so that men can cooperate without constantly fighting over women. Every society needs an orderly way to transfer ownership of property so we won't fight to obtain from others the things we want, etc.

Different cultures have different systems to address the same sins. In some cultures strip clubs are not allowed. In my culture strip clubs are allowed, but not next to a school. In some places, culturally correct ladies cover their legs, chest, and head. In other cultures, ladies cover only their legs and chest, in others only their legs and head. You get the idea. Every culture everywhere has to deal with more or less the same sins, but they do so in a variety of ways. So even though earth's cultures may appear very different, they are alike in this one profoundly important way.

There is, however, one culture that is not in any way involved with sin. How can this be so, since every culture on earth is composed of sinful people? It's because this one culture is not an earthly culture. It is the culture of heaven.

Heaven has a culture? Every group of people in every place in every time has a culture that defines what they do, how they think, and why. Every people in every place in every time. The Bible tells us Jesus' people will be in heaven forever. So yes, heaven has a culture.

But how can we know anything about heaven's culture? And why does it even matter? We actually know quite a bit about heavenly culture. Much of Jesus' teaching was devoted to introducing his disciples to it. Why? He expected them to begin living the culture of heaven while they were on earth. He expects the same of his disciples now. That's why it matters. I know I'm repeating myself, but this bears repeating. Jesus taught us the culture of heaven because he expects us to begin living it now.

But we have a problem. We've already talked about that, too. We're tempted to think Jesus came so that we could live a sort of cleaned-up version of our earthly culture, as if Jesus took our culture's ideal man, showed him how to be an even better father, husband, worker, investor, household finance manager, etc., then held that guy up as our model. We think Jesus came to help us become the guy we always wanted to be anyway. The guy every guy wants to be. Change the pronouns and this is true for women too. We live as if Jesus came to show us a holy pathway to the life everyone in our culture wants.

Do you see the problem with that? We act as if Jesus came to take us to the best version of our earth culture. But he didn't. He came to die so that through his sacrifice we can stand before God and enter heaven. He came to take us to heaven, and he wants us to live like we're there already.

And the ideal man of heaven culture? It's him, of course. Jesus. He is our model. He actually wants us to live like him. I know, I know. We have all sorts of reasons why we can't. But he doesn't care if we think it is impossible. That's still what he wants. Actually, that's what he expects of those who follow him.

Most of Jesus' teaching involved the culture of heaven. He put great effort into helping his followers see the social structure of heaven, how heavenly people think and act, what motivates them and what doesn't, what they believe, who they admire, and how they distinguish between right and wrong, between what is real and what is not. He wasn't making them better. He was making them new. Do you see the difference?

God is not looking for surface-level behavioral change. Instead he's after absolute transformation in our thinking about ourselves, about him, about the world, about everything. This interior transformation will certainly influence our actions, but no mere change in behavior can transform us inside.

God knows that such transformation is beyond the efforts of even the most pious among us. This is why he promised to do it for us, *if* we offer ourselves up completely and quit conforming to our earth culture.

> I appeal to you therefore, brothers, by the mercies of God, *to present your bodies as a living sacrifice*, holy and acceptable to God, which is your spiritual worship. *Do not be conformed to this world, but be transformed by the renewal of your mind*, that by testing you may discern what is the will of God, what is good and acceptable and perfect. Romans 12:1-2

No matter how dramatic our conversion experience, this internal transformation is gradual and progressive. Just ask Paul. His transformation started in Acts 9, but his writings show that it continued for the rest of his life. Our transformations will take the rest of our lives too.

Essentially every aspect of the culture of heaven was counterintuitive for Jesus' disciples initially, and we have the same problem. We've been taught the tenets of our own earth culture so thoroughly that we don't even question most of them. Actually, we don't even notice most of them. They have become so self-evident that they are invisible to us. And their effects on our lives are invisible too. Living the culture of heaven requires us to begin to see these effects and question them. It's always been that way.

The intentional, life-long, Holy Spirit-facilitated adoption of the culture of heaven is one way of understanding what it means to live in the kingdom of God. His kingdom is not founded on race, genealogical descent, economics, or geopolitics, but only on the righteousness of Jesus. It comprises all those everywhere who've been redeemed, are being transformed by the renewing of their minds, and are being taught by the Holy Spirit to live the culture of heaven here on earth.

Jesus taught his disciples to pray in Matthew 6. Take a second to review his model prayer. First, he reminds us that we pray to none other than our holy heavenly

Father. And what is to be our first concern as we address him? Pay close attention here, for this is critically important!

"Your kingdom come, your will be done, on earth as it is in heaven."

Jesus taught that when we speak with our Father our primary concern is to always be his kingdom. We are to pray primarily that his divine will be done on earth as it is already being done in heaven. This model prayer is a prayer about living heaven culture! Those who seek God's heart yearn passionately for the day when Jesus returns and the culture of heaven is finally fully expressed on a new earth. This is the prayer of those who are following Jesus, those who are already living the culture of heaven.

The New Testament is full of teachings about the culture of heaven. Once you start to find them, you'll see them everywhere. The next few pages contain just a few examples from Matthew's gospel.

God sees blessings very differently than most people see blessings. This is because he sees blessedness in the context of heaven culture and we see blessedness in the context of earth culture.

> "Blessed are the poor in spirit, for theirs is the kingdom of heaven. Blessed are those who mourn, for they shall be comforted. Blessed are the meek, for

> they shall inherit the earth. Blessed are those who hunger and thirst for righteousness, for they shall be satisfied. Blessed are the merciful, for they shall receive mercy. Blessed are the pure in heart, for they shall see God. Blessed are the peacemakers, for they shall be called sons of God. Blessed are those who are persecuted for righteousness' sake, for theirs is the kingdom of heaven."
>
> Matt 5:2-10

Earth cultures, even very religious ones, have concepts of holiness. But they are false.

> "For I tell you, unless your righteousness exceeds that of the scribes and Pharisees, you will never enter the kingdom of heaven."
>
> Matt 5:20

Ready for a hard teaching on heaven culture? The pursuit of earthly wealth, a prominent ambition in most earth cultures, has no place in the culture of heaven. In fact, pursuing wealth leads us away from God. It is contrary to the culture of heaven.

"*Do not lay up for yourselves treasures on earth*, where moth and rust destroy and where thieves break in and steal, but lay up for yourselves treasures in heaven, where neither moth nor rust destroy and where thieves do not break in and steal. For where your treasure is, there you heart will be also."

"No one can serve two masters, for either he will hate the one and love the other, or he will be devoted to the one and despise the other. You cannot serve God and money."

"Therefore I tell you, do not be anxious about your life, what you will eat or what you will drink, nor about your body, what you will put on. Is not life more than food, and the body more than clothing? Look at the birds of the air: they neither sow nor reap nor gather into barns, and yet your heavenly Father feeds them. Are you not of more value than they? And which of you by being anxious can add a single hour to his span of life? And why are you anxious about clothing? Consider the lilies of the field, how they grow: they neither toil nor spin, yet I tell you even Solomon in all his glory was not arrayed like one of these. But if God so clothes the grass of the field, which today is alive and tomorrow is thrown into the oven, will he not much more clothe you, O you of little faith? Therefore do not be anxious, saying 'What shall we eat?' or 'What shall we drink?' or 'What shall we wear?' For the Gentiles seek after all these things and your heavenly Father knows that you need them all. But seek first the kingdom of God and all these things will be added to you."

Matt 6:19-21; 6:24-33

"As for what was sown among thorns, this is the one who hears the word, but the cares of the world and the deceitfulness of riches choke the word, and it proves unfruitful."

Matt 13:22

We cannot live the culture of heaven if we allow ourselves to be deceived by riches. This is vexingly hard for us earthlings to believe. We'll talk a lot more about it later. God knows this teaching is hard. In fact, he knows it is impossible to even try to live the culture of heaven without his help. That's why he promises to help all who ask. But there is no such thing as passive asking. We must actively ask.

> "Ask, and it will be given to you; seek, and you will find; knock, and it will be opened to you. For everyone who asks receives, and the one who seeks finds, and to the one who knocks it will be opened." Matt 7:7-8

Sadly, most people won't ask. Jesus said most people will get this wrong. They will drift easily along in the current of their earth culture to their eventual destruction. But he wants his people to be different, to be the few who find the hard way, the narrow gate.

> "Enter by the narrow gate. For the gate is wide and the way is easy that leads to destruction and those who enter by it are many. For the gate is narrow and the way is hard that leads to life, and those who find it are few."
>
> Matt 7:13-14

We cannot simultaneously set our minds on "the things of man," i.e. earth culture, and also on "the things of God," i.e. heaven culture. Jesus repeatedly insists we exclusively aspire to the things of God.

> But he turned and said to Peter, "Get behind me, Satan! You are a hindrance

23

> to me. For you are not setting your
> mind on the things of God, but on the
> things of man."

Matt 16:23

Living the culture of heaven means putting our allegiance to the kingdom of heaven above all other kingdoms. God understands the demands earthly kingdoms make of us. He will help us navigate these earth culture demands in a way that further strengthens our identification with heaven.

> When they came to Capernaum, the
> collectors of the two-drachma tax went
> up to Peter and said, "Does your
> teacher not pay the tax?" He said,
> "Yes." And when he came into the
> house, Jesus spoke to him first, saying
> "What do you think, Simon? From
> whom do kings of the earth take toll or
> tax? From their sons or from others?"
> And when he said, "From others," Jesus
> said to him, "*Then the sons are free*.
> However, not to give offense to them,
> go to the sea and cast a hook and take
> the first fish that comes up, and when
> you open its month you will find a
> shekel. Take that and give it to them for
> me and for yourself."

Matt 17:24-27

In the culture of heaven, the pathway to greatness runs counter to earth culture teachings on greatness.

> "Truly I say to you, unless you turn and become like children, you will never enter the kingdom of heaven. Whoever humbles himself like this child is the greatest in the kingdom of heaven."
>
> Matt 18:3-4

Earth culture teaches us to acquire and treasure exactly those things which prevent us from entering the kingdom of heaven. Our only escape is to disregard earth culture axioms, obey God, and focus on heaven culture.

> The young man said to him, "All these I have kept. What do I still lack?" Jesus said to him, "If you would be perfect, go, sell what you possess and give to the poor, and you will have treasure in heaven: and come, follow me." When the young man heard this he went away sorrowful, for he had great possessions.
>
> And Jesus said to his disciples, "Truly, I say to you, only with difficulty will a rich person enter the kingdom of heaven. Again I tell you, it is easier for a camel to go through the eye of a needle than

for a rich person to enter the kingdom of God." When the disciples heard this, they were greatly astonished, saying, "Who then can be saved?" But Jesus looked at them and said, "With man this is impossible, but with God all things are possible."

Matt 19:20-26

Rank in the culture of heaven derives not from wealth or power, but from sacrificial service.

But Jesus called them to him and said, "You know that the rulers of the Gentiles lord it over them, and their great ones exercise authority over them. It shall not be so among you. But whoever would be great among you must be your servant, and whoever would be first among you must be your slave, even as the Son of Man came not to be served but to serve and to give his life as a ransom for many."

Matt 20:25-28

If you want to *learn* the culture of heaven, *study* what Jesus said. If you want to *live* the culture of heaven, *believe* what Jesus said. Earth culture says we can't live like him and shouldn't even try.

So don't listen to earth culture. Listen to Jesus. Believe what he said is true. Live the culture of heaven.

3

LIVING HEAVEN CULTURE NOW

What happens to people who live as if these teachings were actually true? According to Jesus, they suffer for it. Jesus is the only human to ever fully demonstrate heaven culture while living on earth, and the world treated him roughly. Further, he taught that if we follow him in living the culture of heaven, we too will be treated roughly. He doesn't warn us it *might* happen, he promises us it *will* happen.

This isn't an aspect of our faith that we find attractive. We don't hear sermons about it. We prefer a version of following Jesus that makes our lives on earth more comfortable, not more difficult. We talk about Christian conversion going something like this. A man's life is a mess. He has trouble with relationships, trouble at work, trouble with money, maybe trouble with some addiction, maybe trouble with the law… Then the man begins attending church. There he learns how to be a better husband, a better father, a better worker. He learns how to better manage his money, conquer his addictions, live respectably. People like the changes they see. His life is better. Everyone is happy. The end.

We have a tendency to portray Jesus as a rescuer of those who have strayed from our cultural ideals, one who will gently turn them back toward our culturally-defined "good life," and many primarily see his church as the agency of this redirection. The message becomes something like this. You are unhappy because your life is messed up. Come to church. Get your life straightened out. Then you can be happy. You'll be a "success." Jesus will show you how.

But this isn't what Jesus taught. He didn't come to rehabilitate our lives so that we could be happy. He came to sanctify our lives so that we could be holy. He explicitly warned us that following him would cost us everything, perhaps even our lives. Every follower must choose between these two versions of following Christ, the false or the true. Will he try to use Jesus to achieve the ideals of his earth culture, or will he allow Jesus to lead him into conflict with it? Where do we want to be praised and rewarded, here or in heaven? The culture of heaven is not admired on earth. Those who live it here must be content with the promise of applause in heaven.

Read how Jesus prepared his disciples for this. He knew how their earth culture would react as they followed him into heaven culture. The consolation he gave is unswervingly heaven-focused. It will be worth all the rejection you will experience from living heaven culture on earth, he says, when you are living heaven culture in heaven. When the world treats you roughly, don't forget this promise. You will live in heaven forever. The best blessing now is the promise of blessings to come.

> And he lifted up his eyes on his disciples and said, "Blessed are you who are poor, for yours is the kingdom of God. Blessed are you who are hungry now, for you shall be satisfied. Blessed are you who weep now, for you shall laugh. Blessed are you when people hate you and when they exclude you and revile you and spurn your name as evil, on account of the Son of Man! Rejoice in that day, and leap for joy, for behold, *your reward is great in heaven*; for so their fathers did to the prophets."
>
> Luke 6:20-23

But there many listeners who still assumed that following Jesus would secure their earth culture's "good life" for them. So he made it even clearer for them:

> "But woe to you who are rich, for you have received your consolation. Woe to

you who are full now, for you shall be hungry. Woe to you who laugh now, for you shall mourn and weep. Woe to you when all people speak well of you, for so their fathers did to the false prophets."

Luke 6:24-26

Perhaps you're a bit confused. You may have been taught that being financially secure, well provisioned, happy, and well respected in the community are the very blessings Jesus wants to give his people.

Know this. It wasn't Jesus who taught you that. Here's more of what Jesus taught:

"If they have called the master of the house Beelzebul, how much more will they malign those of his household?"

Matt 10:25

Then Jesus told his disciples, "If anyone would come after me, let him deny himself and take up his cross and follow me. For whoever would save his life will lose it, but *whoever loses his life for my sake will find it*. For what will it profit a man if he gains the whole world and forfeits his soul? Of what shall a man give in return for his soul?"

Matt 16:24-26

"For whoever is ashamed of me *and of my words* in this adulterous and sinful generation, of him will the Son of Man also be ashamed when he comes in the glory of his Father with the holy angels."

Mark 8:38

Jesus said, "Truly I say to you, there is no one who has left house or brothers or sisters or mother or father or children or lands, for my sake and for the gospel, who will not receive a hundredfold now in this time, houses and brothers and sisters and mothers and children and lands, *with persecutions*, and in the age to come eternal life."

Mark 10:29-30

"But be on your guard, for they will deliver you over to councils, and you will be beaten in synagogues, and you will stand before governors and kings for my sake, to bear witness before them. And the gospel must first be proclaimed to all nations. And when they bring you to trial and deliver you over, do not be anxious beforehand what you are to say, but say whatever is given you in that hour, for it is not you who speak, but the Holy Spirit. And brother will deliver brother over to death, and the father his child, and children will rise against parents and have them put to death. And you will be hated by all for my name's sake. But the one who endures to the end will be saved."

Mark 13:9-13

"But I say to you who hear, Love your enemies, do good to those who hate you, bless those who curse you, pray for those who abuse you. To one who strikes you on the cheek, offer the other also, and from one who takes away your cloak do not withhold your tunic either."

Luke 6:27-29

Now great crowds accompanied him and he turned and said to them, "If anyone comes to me and does not hate his own father and mother and wife and brothers and sisters, yes, and even his own life, he cannot be my disciple. *Whoever does not bear his own cross and come after me cannot be my disciple.* For which of you, desiring to build a tower, does not first sit down and count the cost, whether he has enough to complete it? Otherwise, when he has laid a foundation and is not able to finish, all who see it begin to mock him, saying, 'This man began to build and was not able to finish.' Or what king, going out to encounter another king in war, will not sit down first and deliberate whether he is able with ten thousand to meet him who comes against him with twenty thousand? And if not, while the other is a great way off, he sends a delegation and asks for terms of peace. *So therefore any of you who does not renounce all that he has cannot be my disciple."*

Luke 14:25-33

The Pharisees, *who were lovers of money,* heard all these things, and they ridiculed him. And he said to them, "You are those who justify yourselves before men, but God knows your hearts. For *what is exalted before men is an abomination in the sight of God."*

Luke 16:14-15

When Jesus heard this he said to him, "One thing you still lack. Sell all that you have and distribute to the poor, and you will have treasure in heaven; and

35

come, follow me. But when he heard these things, he became very sad, for he was extremely rich. Jesus, seeing that he had become sad, said, "How difficult it is for those who have wealth to enter the kingdom of God."

Luke 18:22-24

"But before all this they will lay their hands on you and persecute you, delivering you up to the synagogues and prisons, and you will be brought before kings and governors for my name's sake. This will be your opportunity to bear witness. Settle it therefore in your minds not to meditate beforehand how to answer, for I will give you a mouth and wisdom, which none of your adversaries will be able to contradict. You will be delivered up by parents and brothers and relatives and friends, *and some of you they will put to death. You will be hated by all for my name's sake*. But not a hair of your head will perish. By your endurance you will gain your lives."

Luke 21:12-19

"If the world hates you, know that it hated me before it hated you. If you were of the world, the world would love you as its own; but because you are not of the world, but I chose you out of the world, therefore the world hates you. Remember the word that I said to you: 'A servant is not greater than his master.' *If they persecuted me, they will also persecute you...*"

John 15:18-20

"I have said these things to you to keep you from falling away. They will put you out of the synagogues. Indeed the hour is coming when whoever kills you will think he is offering service to God. And they will do these things because they have not known the Father, nor me. But I have said these things to you, that when their hour comes you may remember that I told them to you."

John 16:1-4

On the evening of that day, the first day of the week, the doors being locked where the disciples were for fear of the Jews, Jesus came and stood before them and said to them, *"Peace be with you." When he had said this, he showed them his hands and his side.* Then the disciples were glad when they saw the Lord. Jesus said to them again, "Peace be with you. *As the Father has sent me, even so I am sending you.*"

John 20:19-21

These teachings are not the counsel of a savior who came to help us better meet our earth culture's expectations of us. I can't find any promise in scripture that living the culture of heaven will make us fit in better here on earth or make our life here easier. Instead, I find Jesus relentlessly uprooting that notion from the minds of his disciples. Over and over he warns them, and us, that living heaven culture on earth will cause people to hate us, slander us, ridicule us, and physically harm us.

Indeed, there is much reward for those who follow Jesus, and yes, some of it may manifest in this life. But Jesus' repeated promise is that we'll have trouble while in this world. When one day we leave it, however, our troubles will end and we'll enjoy our treasures in heaven forever. This concept is often derided, even in religious circles, as "pie in the sky" theology, as if the only worthwhile pies are ones that can be eaten now. But listen to Jesus. He says sky pie is better.

Paul wrote often about this promise of deferred reward. In I Corinthians 15 he argues against those in the church who didn't believe in the resurrection of believers, i.e. that any reward from following Jesus must come in this life. Paul said "If in Christ we have hope in this life only, then we are of all people most to be pitied." Why? Because those who follow Jesus will suffer in this life! Jesus had said so, and Paul knew it was true. If there are rewards, they must surely come later. Are we satisfied with a promise of after-this-life rewards today? Or do we believe we can only "sell" a Jesus who rewards immediately?

In Paul's transition from persecutor to persecuted in Acts 9, God spoke to Ananias, who wasn't eager to bring the gospel of Jesus to Paul. Ananias seems to have preferred to leave Paul blind and lost. But the Lord said, "Go, for he is a chosen instrument of mine to carry my name before the Gentiles and kings and the children of Israel. *For I will show him how much he must suffer for the sake of my name*." Jesus made no mention of the gospel making Paul's earthly life better. Instead, he spoke of the suffering it would bring him.

And it happened exactly that way. Living heaven culture led Paul to great suffering. But Paul in no way interpreted his suffering as evidence that his life had somehow missed God's blessing. In fact, drawing contrast between his life and that of some false apostles in Corinth, Paul points to his suffering as validating his service to Christ.

> "Are they servants of Christ, I am a better one – I am talking like a madman – with far greater labors, far more imprisonments, with countless beatings, and often near death. Five times I received at the hands of the

Jews the forty lashes minus one. Three times I was beaten with rods. Once I was stoned. Three times I was shipwrecked; a night and day I was adrift at sea; on frequent journeys, in danger from rivers, danger from robbers, danger from my own people, danger from Gentiles, danger in the city, danger in the wilderness, danger at sea, danger from false brothers; in toil and hardship, through many a sleepless night, in hunger and thirst, often without food, in cold and exposure."

II Cor 11:23-27

Paul did not seem to think his suffering extraordinary, as something only for exceptional disciples called to exceptional ministries. In the Philippian letter, he told the church to honor Epaphroditus because he too had risked his life, nearly dying for the work of Christ. Paul also gave them this command in Philippians chapter 3, "Brothers, join in imitating me and keep your eyes on those who walk *according to the example you have in us*." Paul uses his own willingness to suffer as an example to them. Do you remember how the gospel first came to Philippi in Acts 16? If you don't, please pause here and read it again. Paul and Silas had suffered greatly in Philippi. Epaphroditus was simply following Paul's precedent.

We can't be certain that any of the prisoners who heard the gospel from Paul and Silas in that Philippian jail ever became members of the church. We do know that Paul and Silas visited Lydia's household the very next day as they were leaving town, victorious not *despite* their wounds but *because* of them, wounds still fresh, perhaps still bleeding. Paul's suffering for the gospel was well known to the Philippian church from its earliest days.

Years later, Paul wrote this letter to these same brothers and sisters. He was in prison again, this time in Rome. He hadn't compromised his commitment to living out the gospel. His pursuit of the culture of heaven was still bringing him into conflict with the cultures of the world. So when he called these believers to imitate him, they knew he was also calling them to imitate his example of eyes-wide-open suffering for the gospel. It was simply part of the deal, not an unfortunate, unusual aberration.

But that's not all Paul said in Philippians chapter 3. Paul also wanted the church to be discriminating in their imitation, to be very aware of false teachers. He had exemplified for them a mind set on the culture of heaven, along with the suffering associated with living it. But he knew there were many teachers with worldly motivations competing for church influence.

Consider the rest of the passage:

> "Brothers, join in imitating me, and keep your eyes on those who walk according to the example you have in us. For many, of whom I have already told you and now tell you even with tears, walk as enemies of the cross of Christ. Their end is destruction, their god is their belly, and they glory in their shame, with minds set on earthly things."
>
> Phil 3:17-19

He had mentioned these teachers in the first chapter of the letter. Even though some of their teaching was true, their motivation was false. At its base was a desire for earth-culture-inspired personal gain.

> "Some indeed preach Christ from envy and rivalry, but others from good will. The latter do it out of love, knowing that I am put here for the defense of the gospel. *The former proclaim Christ out of selfish ambition*, not sincerely but thinking to afflict me in my imprisonment."
>
> Phil 1:15-17

Paul warned the churches about earth-culture motivated false teachers often. In I Timothy 6:3-10, he wrote that they imagine godliness to be a means of gain, that those who desire to be rich fall into temptation and a snare. In 2 Corinthians he writes: "For we are not, like so many, peddlers of God's word…"

This wasn't an abstract idea to Paul. He wasn't afraid to name names of people in ministry for reasons arising from earth culture. These teachers hadn't offered their bodies as living sacrifices, they hadn't quit conforming to the worldly culture around them, and they weren't being transformed in the thinking of their minds.

So how can believers sort out true teachers from false? One way is to look for suffering. Jesus taught his disciples that unwillingness to suffer for the sheep is one mark of a false shepherd. False teachers won't suffer for Christ. Neither will their disciples. They are like hired hands. Suffering isn't part of their contract.

> "I am the good shepherd. The good shepherd lays down his life for the sheep. He who is a hired hand and not a shepherd, who does not own the sheep, sees the wolf coming and leaves the sheep and flees, and the wolf snatches them and scatters them. He flees because he is a hired hand and cares nothing for the sheep."
>
> John 10:11-13

So then, one way to distinguish true ministers is their willingness to suffer for the gospel. Conversely, one way to distinguish false ministers is their unwillingness to suffer for it. Scripture holds this credential of suffering highly. It is, however, not the type of credential we typically seek when hiring church staff. Might this explain the many ministerial "misfires" that bring dishonor to God's church and his name?

Why would suffering due to living the culture of heaven be such an authenticating marker for ministry? Peter's first letter contains some of the most direct teaching regarding suffering for the gospel in the New Testament. He says we've been called to suffer for doing good, as was Jesus.

> For this is a gracious thing, when, mindful of God, one endures sorrows while suffering unjustly. For what credit is it if, when you sin and are beaten for it, you endure? But if when you do good and suffer for it you endure, this is a gracious thing in the sight of God. *For to this you have been called*, because *Christ also suffered for you, leaving you an example, so that you might follow in his steps*.
>
> I Pet 2:19-21

Jesus suffered for doing good. We will too if we follow his example. We aren't called only to imitate his character, but also his suffering. Beware of those who claim to follow Jesus but will not suffer for him.

I know I've lost some of you. "Not fair!" you protest. "Of course these first-century Christians were suffering! They were being persecuted! You can't compare my life with theirs. I live in a free country!"

I am aware of our Western tendency to dispose of the scriptures above by imagining they apply only to Christians who live under "bad" governments, not to us living in the West, especially not to us in the USA. But scripture makes no such distinction. Jesus says e*veryone* who follows him will suffer.

Maybe we don't suffer because there really isn't much difference between the culture of heaven and our earth culture. Maybe the kingdom of heaven and the United States of America are essentially the same. Maybe that's why we don't suffer. Maybe Jesus wouldn't have suffered either, if he'd just been born here in America like us.

Maybe... But maybe not.

Maybe we don't suffer because we've chosen not to. Maybe we've just written that out of our understanding of following Jesus. Maybe we did so very gradually over such a long period of time that we didn't even realize we'd done it. Maybe we've missed something important.

A wise man once heard me pray. In my prayer I had thanked God that I live in a country where believers aren't persecuted. Afterward he came to me and asked why I'm not being persecuted.

"Because I live in the US," I responded.
"And why do you live in the US?"
"Because I was born here."
"Tell me, if you wanted could you move to a country where Christians are persecuted?"
"I suppose I could, yes."
"Why don't you?"
"Because I don't want to."
"So answer me again. Why are you not being persecuted?"

He had me. I've never forgotten it. Are you following me here? Maybe we're not suffering mainly because we choose to live safely and comfortably. We think that as long as we thank God for letting us do so, it makes everything OK. No one outside the church, and too few inside the church, expect us to ever consider forfeiting our safety to live in a place where our faith might get us in trouble. Much less killed. But Jesus told us to go everywhere, not just the safe places.

Don't misunderstand. One need not travel to a faraway place to suffer for living the culture of heaven. Suffering for the kingdom will find us wherever we are, *if* we choose to live heaven's culture.

But mostly we don't. And because we don't, Jesus' many teachings about suffering don't make much sense to us. So what do we do with them? We apply them to the common sufferings of man: illness, loss, separation, and death. But it doesn't really work. Reread the passages above. God is speaking of suffering that happens uniquely to followers of Jesus *because* they are followers of Jesus. Jesus didn't teach his disciples that they would suffer when they got sick. He didn't need to. Everyone already knew that. He taught that they'd suffer because of him, if they chose to follow him, i.e. to live like he lived. The world won't hate us because we contract cancer. It will hate us because we follow Christ.

So once again, what happens to us if we live the culture of heaven here on earth? We will suffer for it. But remember, we'll only suffer until we die and not a second longer!

Paul taught the Philippian church not only that they would suffer for the sake of Christ, but also that how they react to such suffering is an indicator of a "manner of life worthy of the gospel," i.e. the culture of heaven. They were to remain steadfast, united, and unafraid.

> Only *let your manner of life be worthy of the gospel of Christ*, so that whether I come and see you or am absent, I may hear of you that you are standing firm in one spirit, with one mind striving side by side for the faith of the gospel, and

not frightened in anything by your opponents. This is a clear sign to them of their destruction, but of your salvation, and that from God. For it has been granted to you that for the sake of Christ you should not only believe in him but also suffer for his sake, engaged in the same conflict that you saw I had and now hear that I still have.

Phil 2:27-30

Peter, like Paul, wrote that living the culture of heaven not only provokes suffering, but also governs how we respond to it. Again, we are to respond in a manner that honors Christ.

> Now who is there to harm you if you are zealous for what is good? But even if you should suffer for righteousness' sake, you will be blessed. Have no fear of them, nor be troubled, but in your hearts honor Christ the Lord as holy, always being prepared to make a defense to anyone who asks you for a reason for the hope that is in you [i.e. the hope that is prompting your suffering!]; yet do it with gentleness and respect, having a good conscience, so that when you are slandered, those who revile your good behavior in Christ may be put to shame. For it is better to

suffer for doing good, if that is God's
will, than for doing evil.

I Pet 3:13-17

Peter follows this challenge with a stunning assertion, again evoking the example of Christ. Don't miss this, reader! *This* is the connection between suffering for Christ and true ministry!

> Since therefore Christ suffered in the flesh, arm yourselves with the same way of thinking, *for whoever has suffered in the flesh has ceased from sin*, so as to live for the rest of the time in the flesh no longer for human passions but for the will of God.
>
> I Pet 4:1-2

Read that again: "Whoever has suffered in the flesh *has ceased from sin*…"

The context is clear. Again, he isn't talking about the kind of suffering that is common to mankind: loss of loved ones, painful disease, financial setbacks, or the discomforts associated with an aging body. He is speaking specifically here of the suffering that comes from having "the same way of thinking" as Christ. He's talking about the suffering that is peculiar to those who follow Jesus, the suffering that comes to us when we live the culture of heaven and the world hates us for it, but we keep living heaven culture anyway. Like he did.

But can such suffering cause us to cease from sin, to live the rest of our life on earth not for our human passions but for the will of God?

Yes! You just read it! *You just read exactly that!* Let's examine this a bit more closely.

Pastor Richard Wurmbrand survived fourteen years of torture in a Romanian prison for following Christ, refusing again and again to renounce his faith and give the names of other believers to his torturers. He writes of two kinds of Christians in his book *God's Underground*, "… those who sincerely believe in God and those who, just as sincerely, believe that they believe. You can tell them apart by their actions in decisive moments."

Jesus teaches us to anticipate these "decisive moments." The progressive adoption of the culture of heaven will necessarily lead to conflict with the earth culture surrounding us. At these points we must decide which way we will go. Will we turn back toward the world? Will we attempt to redefine following Jesus and create a religion that doesn't substantially conflict with our cultural ideals? Will we sincerely believe we believe? Or will we look to Jesus, the founder and perfecter of our faith, who for the joy that was set before him endured the cross, despising the shame, and is now seated at the right hand of the throne of God?

> But recall the former days when, after
> you were enlightened, you endured a
> hard struggle with sufferings,
> sometimes being publicly exposed to
> reproach and affliction, and sometimes
> being partners with those so treated.
> For you had compassion on those in
> prison, and you joyfully accepted the
> plundering of your property, since you
> yourselves knew you had a better
> possession and an abiding one.
>
> Hebrews 10:32-34

Backing away from suffering excludes us from fellowship with Christ and with those who, through the ages and around the world, have endured suffering with him and because of him. However, to choose rightly, to move forward faithfully even at these critical points knowing that suffering will surely come from doing so, unites us with this divine fraternity and sets us apart from those who only want a religion which is of benefit in this life. Those faithful ones who, in those decisive moments, choose to suffer in the flesh have broken the fundamental bondage of sin, the fear of death.

Make no mistake. Scripture does not teach that choosing well at such points is only for exceptional disciples like Paul and Peter. It is the only way forward for all those whose only resolve is to please the Father.

Everyone else will back away and turn again toward their earth culture. At their core, they are afraid to end the world's hold on them. They do not wish to cease from sin if doing so comes at such a cost.

> For you have need of endurance, so that when you have done the will of God you may receive what is promised. For "Yet a little while, and the coming one will come and will not delay; but my righteous one shall live by faith, and if he shrinks back, my soul has no pleasure in him." But we are not of those who shrink back and are destroyed, but of those who have faith and preserve their souls.
>
> Hebrews 10:36-39

Did you see it? God finds no pleasure in those who shrink back. They will be destroyed. May we not be numbered among them!

4

GOD'S FAVORITE CULTURE, OUR IDENTITY

Does God have a favorite culture? Yes, but only one. The culture of heaven is his only favorite culture. He doesn't have a second favorite. Let me write that again. No earth culture is God's second favorite.

That's a big idea. Lots of people think that their earth culture must surely be God's favorite. Or at least his second favorite. But they're all wrong. God's only favorite culture is the culture of heaven.

Americans in particular tend to have a problem with this, but we didn't invent the idea that God likes our culture better than any other. Plenty of people over the centuries have had the same idea. In fact, this wrong idea was present at the very beginning of the church. Follow me through a string of events in Acts 6-15. This will take a while but it will be worth it. God thought so. That's why it's in the Bible!

First century Jewish culture was complex. Aramaic-speaking Hebrews made up the majority of the population in Judea. After Jesus' death and resurrection they probably formed the majority of the Jerusalem church and they brought to this church their notion that Jewish culture, especially their version of it, was God's favorite culture.

But there were also Hellenists, Jews who spoke Greek and had probably adopted some other aspects of Greek culture as well. Some of them were born Jews and others were converts to Judaism, and they were spread throughout the Roman Empire. They'd come to Jerusalem to celebrate the Feast of Weeks, had been present for the events of Pentacost, and had heard Peter's sermon. Some of them, too, had come to belief in Christ. So the church at Jerusalem also included a Hellenistic component, probably a minority, and the stage was set for cultural conflict. It began in Acts 6:1.

> Now in these days when the disciples were increasing in number, a complaint by the Hellenists arose against the Hebrews because their widows were being neglected in the daily distribution.

The Hebrew believers thought their Jewish culture was surely God's favorite. To their reckoning, the Hellenists, though also Jewish, weren't Jewish enough to rank in the top tier with them. So the Hebrews favored their widows over the Hellenist widows. Even though these two groups had many cultural similarities, the differences between them were sufficient to spark a conflict that required apostolic intervention. Eventually, seven Hellenists were appointed to supervise the distribution.

If there was any doubt what God thought about putting these Hellenists in positions of authority in the church, he made himself clear over the following chapters. God showed them what he could do with men from this "lesser" culture. Stephen and Philip, two of the seven, became true pioneer heroes of our faith. Stephen became the church's first martyr and Philip its first missionary!

A close observer might have picked up that God's favor seemed to fall on the Hellenists just like it did on the Hebrews. But this was just a taste of what was to come in Acts 10! God, having already shown the church he didn't prefer Hebrew Jews over Hellenist Jews, now would show he didn't prefer Jews over Gentiles!

You remember the story of Peter's trip to Joppa, Cornelius' dream, Peter's dream, Peter's journey to Cornelius' house, and finally the conversion of Cornelius' whole household. I won't copy it here. It would be good to stop and review Acts 10 if you haven't read it recently. Really. Stop and read it again. This is one of the most important milestones in the Bible!

God made it unmistakably evident to Peter that he was bringing Gentiles into his kingdom directly through faith in Jesus. It's hard for us to appreciate today how astonishing this was for Peter and those with him. Luke writes they were "*amazed* because the gift of the Holy Spirit was poured out *even on the Gentiles*."

As Acts 11 begins, these events become well known. Peter comes under criticism from some of the Jewish believers when he returned to Jerusalem. Listen to what they say, "You went to uncircumcised men and ate with them." Yikes! Even eating in Cornelius' Gentile house was unthinkable to these critics! How much more unthinkable to them was inviting this Gentile household into fellowship with God! Peter himself seems almost apologetic, "Who was I that I could stand in God's way?" he asks them.

Don't forget, Peter's critics were believers in Christ. They just didn't understand that heaven culture was different from their earth culture. They'd lived their whole lives believing their culture *was* God's favorite culture. His *only* favorite culture. But now God was consistently showing his church something critically important, that he had no favorite earth culture. He was building his church by creating one new people out of many peoples. And he intended this new people to live a new culture, the culture of heaven.

This was indeed a big idea. It proved too much for some people to swallow. But not everyone. Read on.

Stephen's martyrdom began a period of persecution that scattered believers as far as Phoenicia, Cyprus, and Antioch (Acts 11:19), but most were "speaking the word to no one except Jews." They had missed the importance of Cornelius' conversion. But there were others, notably not natives of Jerusalem, who went as far as Antioch and preached the Lord Jesus to non-Jews also.

This was another breakthrough! Until then, no one except Peter had preached to Gentiles, and as far as we know, Peter had only done it once! But "the hand of the Lord was with them [at Antioch], and a great number who believed turned to the Lord."

As you might imagine, this didn't go unnoticed in the Jerusalem church. They sent a man named Barnabas to investigate. Since brother Barnabas was full of God's Holy Spirit, what he saw gave him great joy. He went to Tarsus to find his friend Saul, the former Pharisee who'd become a believer in Chapter 9, and brought him to Antioch. They stayed in Antioch for a year teaching the new disciples there. The church continued to grow.

A foundational cultural change happened there in Antioch. If you'd asked one of the believers in Jerusalem what his religion was, he'd have told you without hesitation that he was Jewish. Yes, he was a Jew who believed in Jesus, but still he'd have identified himself as a Jew.

But this wasn't true in Antioch. There were believers there who weren't Jewish. They hadn't ever been Jewish. No one in their church was expecting them to become Jewish. So it was that in Antioch the disciples were first called Christians. The church had taken on a new cultural identity. As far as we know from scripture, the church in Antioch was alone in this. But not for long.

In chapter 13, the spirit of God tells the church to set apart Saul (later known as Paul) and Barnabas for a new mission, and the church immediately sends the two out. Upon their return to Antioch after completing this journey, they relayed the crucial observation that God was opening the door of faith to the Gentiles in town after town!

> Then they passed through Pisidia and came to Pamphyllia. And when they had spoken the word of God in Perga, they went down to Attalia, and from there they sailed to Antioch, where they had been commended to the grace of God for the work that they had fulfilled. *And when they arrived and gathered the church together, they declared all that God had done with them, and how he had opened a door of faith to the Gentiles.* And they remained no little time with the disciples.
>
> Acts 14:24-28

What must it have been like for the Antioch church to have heard this report? Imagine the sense of affirmation! They had correctly discerned God's plan to bring Gentiles into the kingdom. They hadn't been mistaken! God was doing everywhere what he had done in Antioch. God was creating a new people. And by following the lead of his Holy Spirit, they found themselves right in the middle of it!

It probably doesn't come as a great surprise, though, that once again not everyone in the Jerusalem church shared in their excitement. In chapter 15 some brothers from Jerusalem came to Antioch and made trouble. They were still convinced that God's favor could only rest on Jews. In their logic, Gentile believers could come to God only by first becoming Jews. Since this conversion involved circumcision, they were called "the circumcision party."

Paul and Barnabas knew better. They'd seen Gentiles come to God through Jesus, not through "Jewishness," and they knew that what the circumcision party was teaching was wrong. So the Antioch church sent them to Jerusalem to report to the church there what they'd seen God do among the Gentiles. This is a curious thing. Peter had already brought the matter of Cornelius' conversion before the Jerusalem church leaders in chapter 11. So adding Gentile believers directly to the family of God without requiring them to first become Jews shouldn't have been a new concept there. But coming to see that your culture isn't God's only favorite culture is just *too* difficult for some people. And changing from living your earth culture to living heaven culture is even *more* difficult!

On the way from Antioch to Jerusalem Paul and Barnabas passed through Phoenicia and Samaria. The churches in these regions received their news with joy. But upon their arrival in Jerusalem, they were again confronted by the circumcision party. Paul and Barnabas didn't debate theology. They simply reported what they'd seen God do among the Gentiles. Eventually their testimony won the day. Jesus' half-brother James, who had become a leader in the Jerusalem church, agreed that the Gentiles turning to the Lord shouldn't be troubled. A letter to that effect was sent back to Antioch. It would seem that would lay the matter to rest. But it didn't. Why? Hold that question. We'll explore it later.

We know that the circumcision party continued to trouble Gentile congregations, preaching that God would only accept Jewish believers. They still believed their culture was God's favorite. They couldn't even perceive the culture of heaven. As the makeup of the church became more and more Gentile, the influence of the circumcision party eventually waned and disappeared. But the influence of people in the church who think their earth culture must surely be God's favorite never went away. We still have them today. And their earth culture allegiance continues to cause trouble.

This problem will never go away. That is why so much New Testament ink is devoted to it. Since it will always be with us, God wants us to know how to combat it. The word "combat" in the previous sentence was chosen intentionally. This will be a fight. We're talking about opposition to the gospel from within the church, from people who love their culture more than they love heaven culture, because they love themselves more than they love Jesus. They seek to justify themselves and their way of life, they don't care if they paralyze the church in the process, and they fight hard.

These people will use Jesus' name and try to hijack his church to promote their earth culture. They may align themselves and their churches with political parties who promise to protect their earth culture, or even restore some nostalgic imagination of it. They may use their pulpits to promote and defend the ideals of their earth culture. They may confound allegiance to their earth culture and allegiance to God. You might even find the flag of an earth country displayed behind their pulpits, a tacit promotion of the idea that their earth culture is God's favorite. Churches controlled by such people show little interest in taking the gospel to the nations, because the gospel has already come to the only nation they love. As far as they are concerned, the others can go to hell as long as they don't bother them on the way. The modern-day circumcision party, like the one in Acts, has a form of godliness, but denies the gospel's power to transform. They don't talk about circumcision now, but they are the direct spiritual descendants of the circumcision party.

Note this well, you don't read about the circumcision party suffering for the kingdom. They preached that others should suffer, but not them. You won't typically see much inclination to suffer for the kingdom among their modern-day counterparts either.

You may have heard of ethnocentrism, the tendency to use our own earth culture as the lens through which we evaluate other earth cultures. It causes all sorts of problems, but it doesn't necessarily kill our souls. If we understand that God's favorite culture is the culture of heaven and not ours, Jesus will lead us past our tendency to see our earth culture as superior to others.

But preferring our earth culture over the culture of heaven is different. To do this is to prefer ourselves and our wisdom to Jesus and his wisdom. This form of ethnocentrism is a deadly spiritual disease. Left untreated, it is uniformly spiritually lethal. But there is good news! There exists a 100% effective treatment.

Paul gave us the prescription in Romans 12:1-2. We must present ourselves as a living sacrifice. We must no longer conform to the world. We must allow God to transform us by renewing our minds. We must live the culture of heaven.

Maybe you're still not quite sure you understand the difference between your earth culture and the culture of heaven. Don't worry, just keep reading. It will get clearer soon.

See if this helps. Let's contrast "success" according to earth culture with success according to the culture of heaven. My particular earth culture worships money. It uses money to measure everything, including people, even using terms like "net worth." Not surprisingly, my culture holds that being successful means accumulating money. Ask most people in my culture who is the most successful person they know, and they will immediately think of the wealthiest person they know.

In my culture, more money = more success.

But heaven culture is different. Can you imagine Jesus describing himself as successful because he had accumulated money? Would he ever describe someone's "net worth" in terms of money? Of course not. Heaven culture worships God, and being successful means bringing glory to God. In heaven culture, Jesus was the most successful person ever to live.

In heaven culture, more glory to God = more success.

Here's how Jesus summarized his life:

> "I glorified you on earth, having accomplished the work that you gave me to do."
>
> John 17:4

Does that help you see the difference? Again, this is no trivial matter! Recognizing the difference is fundamental to following Jesus!

Some of you are still confused. You're asking, "But can't we do both? Can't we be successful both in the eyes of the world and in the eyes of God?"

Nope.

God said this is impossible. And he knows.

Look again at this verse:

> "No one can serve two masters, for either he will love the one and hate the other or be devoted to the one and despise the other. *You cannot serve God and money*."
>
> Matt 6:24

Some will protest, "But here Jesus is condemning *serving* money, not *having* money. Surely a person can have money but not serve it." Actually, no. You can't. Just a few sentences earlier, Jesus had said this:

> "*Do not lay up for yourselves treasures on earth*, where moth and rust destroy and where thieves break in and steal, *but lay up for yourselves treasures in heaven*, where neither moth nor rust destroys and where thieves do not

break in and steal. *For where your treasure is, there your heart will be also."*

Matt 6:19-21

I know some of you are still not convinced. "Really? A person can't have wealth without serving it?" Jesus answered this exact question explicitly and repeatedly. And his answer is consistently no. According to Jesus, it's impossible. Jesus presents this as a binary choice, one of many "Don't do this; do this instead" commands. He was as clear on this point as he could possibly be.

Money pulls our hearts toward the world. Jesus pulls our hearts toward heaven. Our earth culture teaches us to serve money. The culture of heaven teaches us to serve Jesus. We will choose one or we will choose the other. There isn't any provision in scripture for choosing both. The notion that we can simultaneously pursue both doesn't come from Jesus; it contradicts Jesus. It comes from where everything contrary to Jesus comes, our enemy. Satan would like us to believe this impossible thing is not only possible, but honorable and praiseworthy. But it is not honorable, or praiseworthy, or even possible.

Many of us believe that Jesus was speaking in generalities here. We know what scripture says about money, but we think it's only true for *most* people, not exceptional people like us. It was good of Jesus to give this general advice for the masses, we think, but we're among the rare few who can pull it off. Most people can't have treasure on earth and keep their hearts focused on heaven, but we can. Satan knows we like to think that way, and he likes it too. It is a form of pride and it opens us up to him.

Anyone who imagines himself in a dual pursuit of money and heaven is allowing himself to be deceived. He may imagine he is pursuing both God and money, but when God looks at that man he doesn't see a man pursuing God and money, he just sees a man pursuing money. Remember, God says it is impossible to pursue both. We will either aspire to God and his value system or aspire to the world and its value system. Heaven culture or earth culture. One or the other. So humble yourself before the Lord. Believe he knows more about these matters than even an exceptional person like you. Submit to his wisdom and his lordship. Determine to seek only him.

> You adulterous people! Do you not know that friendship with the world is enmity with God? Therefore whoever wishes to be a friend of the world makes himself an enemy of God.
>
> James 4.4

James calls this imaginary dual pursuit "double mindedness." He doesn't have anything good to say about it.

> If any of you lack wisdom, let him ask God, who gives generously to all without reproach, and it will be given him. But let him ask in faith, with no doubting, for the one who doubts is like a wave of the sea that is driven and tossed by the wind. For that person must not suppose that he will receive anything from the Lord; he is a double-minded man, unstable in all his ways.
>
> James 1:5-8

Listen to what James is saying. Doubting isn't merely lack of faith in God's promises. It is double-mindedness. It is trying to reconcile God's promises with the world's promises so that we can pursue both.

To doubt is to allow faith in the world and its wisdom to compete with faith in God and his wisdom. God doesn't reward that. He doesn't give double-minded people anything. It's as simple as that. God demands our single-minded pursuit.

But don't miss the promise here. If we choose to pursue him single-mindedly, God *generously* gives us wisdom! What is this wisdom? A new way of thinking, *his* way of thinking, along with a new way of living, complete with a new set of values and aspirations. Complete transformation. A whole new heavenly culture.

Those who abandon double-mindedness can expect God to guide them into his culture. God knows this is not easy, therefore he gives his wisdom to the single-minded without reproaching them. He knows they will suffer plenty of reproach from the world.

Is there, then, hope for the double-minded? Absolutely, *if* they turn away from the world and toward the Lord, and set themselves single-mindedly to removing earth culture from their hearts.

> Draw near to God and he will draw near to you. Cleanse your hands, you sinners, and purify your hearts, you double-minded.
>
> James 4:8

Here's the real question. What do you desire most of all? If everything in your life could be just the way you want it to be, how would your life look?

Scripture speaks of people having heaven-derived desires and aspirations.

> My desire is to depart and be with Christ, for that is far better.
>
> Phil 1:23

> ... they desire a better country, that is a heavenly one.
>
> Hebrews 11:16

> For here we have no lasting city, but we
> seek the city that is to come.
>
> Hebrews 13:14

But most verses that mention "desiring" or "seeking after" are warnings against earth culture aspirations. Some of these worldly desires are obviously non-heavenly, like sexual immorality. But some earth-derived desires are much more subtle.

Remember the parable of the sower? He sowed seed in four different soils. The third soil contained so many thorns that when the seed sprouted and grew, the thorns choked it and it yielded no grain. None at all. How did Jesus interpret this soil?

> "...They are the ones who hear the word, but the *cares of the world* and the *deceitfulness of riches* and the *desires for other things* come in and choke the word, and it proves unfruitful."
>
> Mark 4:18-19

Listen carefully to what Jesus said. Three thorns choke the word in the lives of these people: worldly cares, deceitful riches, and desires for other things. All three thorns are elements of earth culture. We can't live both earth culture and heaven culture. If we try to do so, earth culture will always win. In that case, Jesus said, the word he sowed in us will prove unfruitful.

Let's look at the thorns one by one. What are these "cares of the world?" The Greek word used here is common in the NT. It comes from a verb usually translated "to worry" or "to be anxious." In Matthew 6, Jesus tells us not to worry about our life, what we will eat or drink or wear. He tells us not to worry about tomorrow. It's the same verb. In Matthew 10:19 Jesus tells us not to worry how to respond to our persecutors. In Luke 10:41 Jesus tells Martha she is worried and troubled about many things.

The world would have us believe there are concerns which merit worrying and concerns which don't, therefore we should save our worrying for the big, important things. We all know the worldly proverb "Don't sweat the small stuff!" But surely food and water are big things! So is Jesus telling us not to worry about big things either? Yes. That is exactly what he is saying.

Worrying, no matter what we're worried about, is earth culture. In Philippians 4:6, Paul simply tells us not to worry about anything, instead we are to pray. There is no worry in heaven. If we live earth culture, the thorns of worry, the "cares of the world," will coil around us tighter and tighter until they eventually make us unfruitful. Spiritual dead ends. So to live heaven culture is to live without worry.

The best solution earth culture can offer to worries is money. If you have enough money, you won't have to worry about what is coming next, what you will eat or drink or wear. You can feast in front of your overflowing barn and laugh at tomorrow. And who will persecute you if you are rich? Get enough money, says earth culture, and you won't have to worry about anything. But it's a lie, a deception.

That leads us to the deceitfulness of riches, the second thorn mentioned in the parable. One need not be rich to succumb to money's deceit. Wealth is an equal-opportunity deceiver. Here's how the deception works. A man worries about tomorrow. So he gathers money. But still he worries. "I must not yet have enough money," he reasons. So he gathers more money. But tomorrow still doesn't seem as secure as he imagined it would, so he gathers yet more money, and on the story goes. "Enough money" is a shifting mirage. And so the thorny vine tightens and tightens.

But the most insidious thorn is the third, the desire for other things. What other things? *Any* other things. As mentioned earlier, the New Testament uses the word desire often, but usually in a negative sense. John sums them up this way:

> And the world is passing away along
> with its desires, but whoever does the
> will of God abides forever.
>
> I John 2:17

Any desire other than doing the will of God is a thorn. To live the culture of heaven is to live in absolute and exclusive submission to the will of God. To desire God along with any other desires is to live earth culture. He's not hoping to be high on our list of desires, not even top of the list. He demands to *be* our list.

We tend not to believe Jesus here. We all carry a list of "other things" that compete with our desire to do the will of God. Some are evil, but some are good. Evil or good is not the issue. The issue is singlemindedness.

Here's an example. What could be purer than a believer's desire to be in heaven with Christ Jesus? Nevertheless, even this good desire competed with doing the will of God in Paul's heart. Listen to him struggle.

> I am hard pressed between the two. My desire is to depart and be with Christ, for that is far better. But to remain in the flesh is more necessary on your [the Philippian church's] account. Convinced of this, I know that I will remain and continue with you all, for your progress and joy in the faith,…
>
> Phil 1:23-25

Even Paul's intense longing for heaven could have been an obstacle to his obedience to God's purpose for him. He had to subjugate even that Godly desire to his service to the Lord. So must all of us put even our best and noblest desires, like being a good parent or a good spouse, in the context of God's unlimited lordship over us. Otherwise, even these excellent desires become thorns which strangle our souls into unfruitfulness. Jesus told us to pray "May your will be done on earth as it is in heaven." God's will is already done in heaven. To live heaven culture here on earth, we must desire nothing here other than to play our part in his unfolding story. *Simple*. Living heaven culture is not easy, but it *is* simple.

Jesus tells us to seek God's kingdom, to not worry like the world does. We are not to be taken in by the deception of wealth, as is the world. And we are to desire God's will and nothing else. This is the thorn-free culture of heaven. But living this culture is not natural for us, nor is it a "once and for all" matter.

Thorns are not easily overcome. I grew up surrounded by Kentucky countryside. One of our childhood summertime passions was wild blackberries. They grew on thorny vines in fencerows everywhere and we picked gallons of them. Why? Because there is simply no food on earth like a freshly buttered oven-hot biscuit topped with blackberry jam! (Please God, let there be biscuits and blackberries in heaven!)

A few years ago we bought a house in town. The house was fine except for one thing. No blackberry vines. So I went out to my parents' place one day, dug up some vines and planted them in my yard. That was not the smartest thing I've ever done.

True, I now have blackberries right outside my door, but these vines spread so aggressively I wonder if one summer night they'll surround the house, creep in the window, and strangle us in our sleep. I've decided to cut them down next spring, but I know they won't give up. I'll have to be vigilant for their sprouting progeny from now on. So will whoever owns this house after me. And whoever owns it after them, I'm afraid. So it is with the thorns in the parable. They'll keep looking for their chance to strangle us. If it was a constant struggle for Paul, it will be for us as well.

I know I've already written a lot about money, but so did God. Here's a bit more. Scripture warns us about accumulating wealth, but not against earning money. There aren't any scriptures warning against having a good-paying job. It's what we do with the money we earn that gets us into trouble. Paul told the Ephesian believers to do honest work with their hands *so that they would have something to share with others* (Eph 4:28). To the Corinthians Paul writes "You will be enriched in every way *to be generous in every way*..." (2 Cor 9:11).

Religious rich people often defend their wealth by pointing out rich believers in the New Testament. But in each case, these wealthy disciples are mentioned in the positive context of giving their money away or the negative context of refusing to do so. We can hoard our excess money, or we can be obedient by giving it. But where is the dividing line between what we keep and what we share? Look at Jesus' example.

> For you know the grace of our Lord
> Jesus Christ, that though he was rich,
> yet for your sake he became poor, so
> that you by his poverty might become
> rich.
>
> II Cor 8:9

That's where Jesus drew the line. He traded riches for poverty for our sakes. If we work so that we can have more for ourselves, that's earth culture. If we work so that we can have more to give, that's heaven culture.

One more quick point. We mustn't think we can whitewash the pursuit of wealth by tithing. Remember the rich young man in Matthew 19? We read about him on page 25. He said he'd kept all the commandments, so he would have been tithing. He had likely been taught that 10% of his income belonged to God, but the remaining 90% belonged to him. Presumably then, the wealth that ultimately kept him from following Jesus came from "his" 90%. Do you see the problem?

Suppose there is a man who doesn't tithe. He uses 100% of his income to pursue wealth. Beside him is another man who tithes. If he uses 90% of his income to pursue wealth, both men have precisely the same problem. Having wealth we believe is ours is earth culture. Understanding that *everything* belongs to God is heaven culture.

Jesus knows about heaven and he knows about money. We should believe what he said about them.

But living the culture of heaven isn't only a matter of avoiding the thorns of earth culture. It is also a matter of identity.

All of us have multiple identities. I am simultaneously a grandfather and a son. Which of these identities is most important depends on the context. My baby grandson doesn't really care that I'm my mother's son and my memory-impaired mother doesn't really care that I'm my grandson's grandfather. My primary identity depends somewhat upon whom I'm with and what I'm doing. It's true for all of us.

Or so it would seem, but be careful here! There is one identity that must always be above every other. Jesus was crystal clear about this. He said whoever comes to him but doesn't hate his own family cannot be his disciple. He wasn't teaching us to hate our families, he was teaching us that we must *primarily* identify ourselves as his disciples. He won't allow identity with him to compete with even the most fundamental, primal earthly identity of all, family kinship. He says those who primarily identify other than as his disciple cannot be his disciple.

If our identification with Christ trumps even our identification with our earthly family, how much more must it trump our identification with our earthly country? Consider this pair of identities. I'm a citizen of the US and I'm also a citizen of heaven. Does context determine which of these is most important?

If so, what would be the context that puts heavenly citizenship more important? Judgment day, maybe? Would that make my American identity more important up until I die? I submit that scripture teaches us to primarily identify as citizens of heaven from the moment we come under the lordship of Christ and forever after.

I'm trying to think of myself as a citizen of heaven who, through no virtue of his own, has an American passport. I like my American passport very much. But like every other benefit arising from my earthly citizenship, I need to consider how to best turn my passport to God's use. It's his after all. When I identify primarily as a citizen of the US, I tend to think mostly about how my US citizenship benefits me. When I identify primarily as a citizen of heaven, I tend to think about how my US citizenship benefits God's kingdom.

Are you a Christian American or an American Christian? Do you see the difference? Try this quick self-test. Do you more easily identify with non-believing Americans or with non-American believers? If you admit to the former, you've got a problem. Many American followers of Jesus have that same problem. For them, the above question wouldn't even make sense.

Here's another self-test question. Has anyone recently asked you to give an account for the hope within you? This is a question that a heaven-identified life should prompt.

> But even if you should suffer for righteousness' sake, you will be blessed. Have no fear of them, nor be troubled, but in your hearts honor Christ the Lord as holy, *always being prepared to make a defense to anyone who asks you for a reason for the hope that is in you*, having a good conscience, so that, when you are slandered, those who revile your good behavior in Christ may be put to shame.
>
> I Peter 3:13-16

Again, has anyone asked you lately to account for your hope? It's not a question I often get either. I wonder why. Maybe it's because I avoid suffering for righteousness' sake. Maybe it's because my imitation of Christ is casual. Maybe my primary identification isn't clear.

Maybe it's because, despite all my religious activity, I basically want the same things the world around me wants. Maybe I just want to be safe and secure and happy and die with money in the bank. Maybe all I want from Jesus is for him to help me get the very same things the world wants.

Maybe my neighbors aren't confused by my life because it doesn't seem much different from theirs. Maybe they aren't intrigued by what is driving me. Maybe the way I live doesn't suggest there's much difference between my identity and theirs, between my hope and their hope. Maybe that's why they rarely ask me to explain anything.

Look how heaven-culture identification "connects the dots" of God's great ambition. Read Eph 3:4-10, remembering that to Paul the word "Gentiles" meant all the non-Jewish peoples of the world.

> When you read this, you can perceive my insight into the mystery of Christ, which was not made known to the sons of men in other generations as it has now been revealed to his holy apostles and prophets by the Spirit. This mystery is that the Gentiles are fellow heirs, members of the same body, and partakers of the promise in Christ Jesus through the gospel. Of this gospel I was made a minister according to the gift of God's grace, which was given me by the working of his power. To me, though I am the very least of all the saints, this grace was given, to preach to the Gentiles the unsearchable riches of Christ, and to bring to light for everyone what is the plan of the mystery hidden for ages in God who created all things, so that through the church the manifold

wisdom of God might now be made known to the rulers and authorities in the heavenly places.

So there you have it. In opening the door of heaven to all people who believe in Jesus, whoever they are, wherever they are, whatever their earth culture was, God is doing something magnificent in his own eyes. He is distinguishing himself from the myriad tribal deities created by earth's peoples. God, who created the earth and everything in it, cannot be possessed.

Instead, through the sacrifice of Jesus, he is creating a new people out of earth's many peoples. He is putting his wisdom and power on display for heaven and earth to see, "Look at what I am doing here!" he commands even the heavenly beings, "Who could do this but me?" From every tribe on earth, God is bringing together a new people who identify more strongly with his kingdom than with any earthly kingdom, a nation of priests, a new people whose culture is the culture of heaven.

Only this divinely created heaven-identified people will glorify God as he has chosen to be glorified. Only they will display his heart for all nations. Only they will sacrificially welcome strangers in Jesus' name without fear or devote themselves to sacrificially bringing the gospel of Christ to culturally distant peoples. Only they will pursue his redemptive mission to all men everywhere (Acts 17:30). People who primarily identity with an earth culture, *any* earth culture, can't properly glorify God. Even if they could, they wouldn't.

We can't talk about identifying with heaven without some discussion of what it means to simultaneously be subject to earthly governments. We've mentioned that we must hold our allegiance to God higher than any other allegiance. So what, then, do we do with Romans 13 and I Peter 2?

These passages seem to say that since God ordained earthly authority we must always obey earthly rulers and earthly laws out of reverence for God. But how do we reconcile obedience to God and obedience to earthly authority when they sometimes seem to be pointing us in opposite directions?

> Let every person be subject to the governing authorities. For there is no authority except from God and those that exist have been instituted by God. Therefore whoever resists the authorities resists what God has appointed, and those who resist will incur judgment. For rulers are not a terror to good conduct, but to bad. Would you have no fear of the one in authority? Then do what is good and you will receive his approval, for he is God's servant for your good. But if you

do wrong, be afraid, for he does not bear the sword in vain. For he is the servant of God, an avenger who carries out God's wrath on the wrongdoer. Therefore one must be in subjection, not only to avoid God's wrath but also for the sake of conscience. For because of this you also pay taxes, for the authorities are servants of God, attending to this very thing. Pay to all what is owed to them: taxes to whom taxes are owed, revenue to whom revenue is owed, respect to whom respect is owed, honor to whom honor is owed.

Rom 13:1-7

Be subject for the Lord's sake to every human institution, whether it be to the emperor as supreme, or to governors as sent by him to punish those who do evil and to praise those who do good.

I Pet 2:13-14

We read these passages, but at the same time we've heard of Christians who live in places where obedience to Christ's commands is illegal. We know of governments which persecute believers and ruthlessly seek to eradicate Jesus' church from their lands. We applaud the courage of brothers and sisters whose obedience to God requires them to disobey such authorities, knowing they will be punished for doing so. This applause emanates from the Holy Spirit and is appropriate. Few of us believe Christians living under such governments should allow earthly authority to define heavenly obedience for them. But are these Christians living outside the tenets of Romans 13 and I Peter 2?

Further, we know earthly authorities are not reliable guides to God's heart. We see it with our own eyes, and we read it in scripture over and over. What about Pharaoh ordering the infanticide of the Hebrew boys (Exodus 1:16)? What about King Herod ordering the murder of the boys in Bethlehem (Matt 2:16)? How many ungodly kings do we find in Kings and Chronicles? So how can we reconcile these instances with Romans and I Peter?

Any time we are faced with such a quandary our best strategy is to imitate Jesus. If obedience to all earthly authorities in all times and places is what God expects of us, it must have been what God expected of Jesus as well. After all, we are called to walk as he walked. So let's see how he walked this.

Are you ready? Here it is. Jesus obeyed the Father. Only the Father. All the time. Period. Sometimes his obedience to the Father brought him into conflict with earthly authorities. When it did, he chose to *place himself in subjection* to these authorities *while continuing to obey the Father*. He didn't resist the authorities or circumvent them or seek to depose them. He chose to be subject to them and accept the consequences. He wasn't being insolent when addressing Pilate. He was giving us a path to follow.

> So Pilate said to him, "You will not speak to me? Do you not know that I have authority to release you and authority to crucify you?" Jesus answered him, "You would have no authority over me at all unless it had been given you from above."
>
> John 19:10-11a

There's the key. Jesus understood that Pilate's authority had come from God, even though he also knew that Pilate was soon to misuse his authority. Nonetheless, Jesus placed himself in subjection to Pilate's poor judgment. Jesus suffered at the hands of misused earthly authority. That's our model. That's Jesus' take on Romans 13 and I Peter 2.

Beware of men who excuse disobedience to God by hiding behind obedience to earthly governments. That's not God's point in Romans 13 and I Peter 2. He is not calling us to cowardice but to courage. Beware also of men in authority who say that obeying man's law equals obeying God's law. That also is not the point God is making. Not every worldly leader lives up to God's standards in Romans 13 and I Peter 2. God does not expect us to obey leaders whose expectations of us conflict with his, he only expects us to be subject to them. Remember the Hebrew midwives who disobeyed Pharoah because they feared God? God didn't scold them. He blessed them with families of their own.

Remember also the refrain of the chief priests before Pilate, "We have no king but Caesar!" God remembers it too. May he never hear such words from us!

5
WHAT ABOUT YOUR CHURCH?

We Americans have a tendency toward personalizing every scriptural teaching. It's a part of our very individualistic American earth culture, and we bring it to church with us. Part of our problem is the English language, since our second-person pronoun "you" can be either singular or plural. Commands to individuals and commands to groups can sound the same in English. Southerners cleverly solve the problem with our word y'all. I don't know what the rest of y'all do.

But most commands in scripture were given to *all of us together*, not to *each of us individually*. Individualizing everything can cause us to miss the sense of instructions intended for the whole church. It isn't only individuals who must choose heaven's culture over our earth culture, we must do so as churches as well. This is a big deal. We can't live heaven culture individually while living earth culture collectively as church.

Individual piety is not all God wants from us. Everything your church does, says, and thinks must be examined in light of whether it promotes earth culture or heaven culture. Those in leadership must relentlessly ask themselves "Does this aspect of our church's life derive from earth or from heaven?" Every motivation, every aspiration, everything the church holds up as praiseworthy or admirable must pass through that filter before it is endorsed, even tacitly, by church leaders before the body of believers. Every single thing. Every single time. It's hard work! Many churches haven't been sufficiently careful with this.

But there's more! It isn't enough to teach heaven culture, we need to follow Jesus' example and "unteach" earth culture as well. Teaching heaven culture *may* tick people off. But unteaching earth culture *will* tick them off nearly every time. Especially people who should know better.

For one thing, it's at odds with the attractional model of church growth. Will anyone want to join a church corporately living the culture of heaven and enduring the attendant suffering? Even more to the point, how many current members will leave if we start expecting each other to live like Jesus? But such questions miss the mark. Jesus expects us to imitate him, not market him. Marketing is earth culture. If we operate the church like a business instead of an outpost of heaven, we shouldn't be surprised when members act like customers instead of disciples.

Being an "unearthly" church requires more wisdom than the even wisest among us possess. God knows that. Again, that's why he promises us his Holy Spirit. Some church leaders are tempted to look to earth culture, particularly the business world, for counsel. But only God himself can help us know and reflect his heart. Jesus' last pre-crucifixion evening with the disciples, the ones through whom he would soon build his church, contained many assurances of divine help in this regard. Only God has the wisdom we need to build a heaven-culture church. Notice the past, present, and future aspects of the Holy Spirit's help promised in the following verses.

> "These things I have spoken to you while I am still with you. But the Helper, the Holy Spirit, whom the Father will send in my name, he will teach you all things and *will bring to your remembrance all that I have said* to you.

> "But when the helper comes, whom I will send to you from the Father, the Spirit of Truth, who proceeds from the Father, *he will bear witness about me*."

> "I still have many things to say to you, but you cannot bear them now. When the Spirit of truth comes, he will guide you into all the truth, for he will not

speak on his own authority, but whatever he hears he will speak, and *he will declare to you the things that are to come.*"

John 14:25-26; 15:26; 16:12-13

God knows the pressure on churches to conform to the expectations of earth culture is almost overwhelming. Allowing God to transform everything worldly about her, i.e. having her adopt heaven's culture, is much harder than crafting fine sermons, polishing bright Sunday services, or organizing thoughtful programming. But this totally transformative cleansing is exactly what Jesus knows his church needs.

> Husbands, love your wives, as Christ loved the church and gave himself up for her, that he might sanctify her, having cleansed her by the washing of water with the word, so that he might present the church to himself in splendor, without spot or wrinkle or any such thing, that she might be holy and without blemish.

Eph 5:25-27

Churches resisting this transformation by fearfully clinging to earth-culture models of human organizations, will invariably become agencies of their earth culture, using "a form of godliness" to promote earth culture ideals while denying the gospel's power to transform believers into citizens of heaven. No church can serve both God's ideals and those of her earth culture. Eventually churches who try will become salt which has lost its saltiness, ready only to be thrown out. Their main use to God at that point is as a bad example.

> "You are the salt of the earth, but if salt has lost its taste, how can it be restored? It is no longer good for anything except to be thrown out and trampled under people's feet."
>
> Matt 5:13

I work for a nonprofit that helps churches welcome "strangers" coming to our community (Matt 25:31-46). God expects his people to welcome strangers. He told us clearly in scripture after scripture. But where I live, churches sometimes need a little reminder. Even with the reminder, some still refuse to obey. I remember explaining the mandate to welcome to a fellow believer once. After scripturally tracing this aspect of God's heart and his clear commands in both Old and New Testaments, she said "James, you've convinced me welcoming strangers is a good thing in God's sight… But do you really think it's *wise*?"

Do you see what was behind her question? Scripture had convinced her that God expects his people to welcome strangers. But that wasn't enough for her. Before she embraced this truth she acknowledged, she needed to filter it through earth culture-informed notions of wisdom. Before she obeyed God, she wanted to be sure obeying was going to benefit her (and her earthly nation) in this life. She had it exactly backwards.

Dear sister, our obedience to God will seem wise to people in heaven later, whether or not it seems wise to people on earth now. Always think heaven. Live heaven. Live heaven culture now. Any "wisdom" to the contrary won't seem so wise later!

But don't be an individualistic American here, reader. Don't focus only on this sister. Focus on her church, in which she is deeply involved. It was her church who taught her what following Jesus means and doesn't mean. It was her church who held no expectation she would primarily identify with the culture of heaven. I know something of this church. In meetings where critical decisions are being made, the leaders are asking the same "Yes, but is it wise?" question. She was only reflecting her church.

In this sister's case, the abrogation of duty by her church was subtle. In some cases it is much more blatant. The online version of Smithsonian Magazine published an article on 1/4/19 entitled "Heavily Abridged 'Slave Bible' Removed Passages That Might Encourage Uprisings." The article describes efforts by 19th century British missionaries to bring the gospel to Caribbean slaves. The slave owners didn't want the missionaries there. So to appease them, the missionaries crafted a "Slave Bible" by carefully editing scripture to omit any passages which might incite a slave rebellion.

All references to Moses leading the Israelites out of Egypt were removed, along with passages such as Jeremiah 22:13: "Woe unto him who buildeth his house by unrighteousness, and his chambers by wrong; that useth his neighbour's service without wages and giveth him not for his work." Also missing was Exodus 21:16: "And he that stealeth a man, and selleth him, or if he be found in his hand, he shall surely be put to death." But here's the problem. The efforts of these missionaries to make the gospel fit inside an earth culture, though obviously wrong to us, were not obviously wrong to them - or to their church. It's always easier to see someone else's error than it is to see your own.

My own great-great-grandfather was both a slaveholder and church leader. How a man could have not noticed the discordance between the culture of heaven and this aspect of his earth culture is astonishing. Maybe he *did* notice but navigated the dilemma to his church's satisfaction. Maybe the problem was that no one in the church expected him to imitate Jesus. Again, it's easy for us to see their error now but I'm guessing nobody in his church saw it then.

Here's another example. In 2006 my wife and I came to believe God wanted us to serve as missionaries in West Africa along with our six youngest children. Many local church people were perplexed by this decision.

Although they knew we were a churchgoing family, they didn't see why we couldn't be more sensible about our religion. Why did we have to get "plumb carried away" with it? What about my medical practice? What about our children? It was contrary to earth culture. Even "Christian" earth culture.

One conversation encapsulated the problem they were having. An older sister asked me why I would want to do such an obviously foolish thing. I told her I was just trying my best to follow Jesus. "Well, just be careful with that!" she retorted. "You remember what happened to *him* don't you?"

Wow! That's it. That's "Christian" earth culture in a nutshell.

This sister had tailored her notion of a "Christian life" so carefully that it fit completely with her earth cultural ideals. Nothing about it challenged any aspect of her earth culture-defined "good life." *Actually, in her mind Jesus himself wasn't a good example of a Christian life!* After all, look what happened to him! Is that really what you want, James?

But again, don't just think about this lady. Think about the church where she was a Sunday School teacher for decades, the church that never challenged the earth culture she brought to church with her every Sunday, the church that never expected her to live the culture of heaven if it meant sacrificing success in the eyes of the world. Her church let her down. Her church let Jesus down.

What does God do with people like her? I can only trust that God's grace is sufficiently expansive to cover both her sins and mine. But again, here's the better question. What does God do with churches like hers? I hate to say it, but I don't see him doing much with them at all. Which is probably fine with them.

So what culture does *your* church promote? Here are some questions to consider. This is by no means a comprehensive exam, just a quick little quiz!

How is your church shaping members' notions of a "successful" life?

Plenty of church people ask Jesus to help them be "successful" in their earth culture, but few ask Jesus to help them be successful in the culture of heaven. Why is that?

Our aspirations are fundamental to everything we do. Sadly, many aspirations come from our earth culture. Ideally, God uses our churches to replace these earthly aspirations with the aspirations of Jesus. That's what transformation is all about. But listen to how the phrase "a successful man" is used in your church meetings. If you can replace it with "a wealthy man," your church has a problem. Jesus didn't measure success by counting money. That's earth culture. It has plenty of advocates. Your church must advocate heaven culture.

Does your church advocate living a "balanced" life?

Beware of "balance." Jesus didn't preach balancing your life. Jesus didn't give us an example of a "balanced" life. He didn't balance obeying God against anything. Neither did Paul and neither should we.

> Brothers I do not consider that I have made it my own. *But one thing I do*: Forgetting what lies behind and straining forward to what lies ahead, I press on toward the goal...
>
> Phil 3:13-14a

Jesus doesn't want us to live a balanced life. Jesus wants us to live like him, for him, and with him. If your church expects any less of you, then you should expect more of your church.

Jesus commissioned his church to go into all the world and make disciples. How is your church participating in this? How many of your own members have you sent? Could you possibly send more?

Consider these two numbers: 400,000 and 12,000,000. Remember them. They show what motivated sending looks like. 400,000 is the number of Americans wearing a military uniform on Dec 7, 1941, the day Pearl Harbor was attacked. 12,000,000 is the number of Americans in uniform 3 ½ years later when World War II ended. Prior to the Pearl Harbor attack Americans knew there was a war, but most of us believed it was someone else's war.

When it suddenly became *our* war, we rapidly increased the size of our military *by a factor of 30*! By war's end, one in twelve Americans were in uniform. Those not in uniform were active participants in the war effort too, in all sorts of sacrificial ways. Maximum collective effort. This is an example of mobilization familiar to us in the US.

But what about your church? Is she totally mobilized to make disciples of all nations? Is she making maximum effort to send as many gospel soldiers as possible to spiritually dark places where the gospel has not yet been heard? Are those in your church who stay just as sacrificially involved in this spiritual war as those who go? Does your church see God's mission as her mission too? Or is your church only vaguely aware of a spiritual war somewhere far away, a war that doesn't seem to threaten her and therefore need not involve her?

Does your church send more members overseas in military uniform than members overseas in mission? Why does our country understand extreme mobilization better than our churches?

We've talked about the problem of double-mindedness at the individual level. Church-level double-mindedness is a problem too. Jesus set one great task before his church. Churches who pursue it single-mindedly make sure everything they do and teach fits within this one context. Let's focus on the one great ambition Jesus has for his church, and make it ours as well!

> And Jesus came and said to them, "All authority in heaven and on earth has been given to me. Go therefore and make disciples of all nations, baptizing them in the name of the Father and of the Son and of the Holy Spirit, and teaching them to observe all that I have commanded you. And behold, I am with you always, to the end of the age."
>
> Matt 28:18-20

Please understand this. Your church can't engage this command with weeklong trips alone. Consider Jesus' trip to earth. He stayed here many years. He learned to speak the language and navigate the culture to which he was sent. Your church needs to be sending people ready to do the same. Having people willing to give up a week of vacation is good, but does your church have people ready to give up a career? Short-term sending is a useful adjunct to long-term sending, but it is no replacement. If your church's sending is largely confined to short-termers, there are underlying earth culture reasons. Look for them.

Does your church have members who are risking their lives for the work of Christ? If not, why not? If so, does she honor them?

> So receive him [Epaphroditus] in the Lord with all joy, and honor such men, for he nearly died for the work of Christ,

> *risking his life* to complete what was
> lacking in your service to me [Paul].
>> Phil 2:29-30

One way to inspire people to live the culture of heaven without shrinking back is to publically honor those like Epaphroditus. Remember, scripture tells us to keep our eyes on those who follow Paul's dangerous example (Phil 3:17). Do you honor those like Epaphroditus among you? If your church hasn't produced any who live in such a way, what does that tell you about the culture of your church? Should that not be a matter of concern?

Is your church led by men whose imitation of Christ is worthy of imitation?

Advocating personal imitation is hard for us for all sorts of reasons, but it's so important!

> So I exhort the elders among you, as a fellow elder and as a witness of the sufferings of Christ, as well as a partaker in the glory that is going to be revealed: shepherd the flock of God that is among you, exercising oversight, not under compulsion, but willingly, as God would have you; not for shameful gain but eagerly, not domineering over those in your charge, *but being examples to the flock*. And when the

> chief Shepherd appears, you will
> receive the unfading crown of glory.
>
> I Pet 5:1-4

Paul understood the power of imitation. He told his readers to imitate him as he imitated Christ (1 Cor 11:1). He even told them to imitate those who imitated him (Phil 3:17). He understood that having believers closely examine and model their lives after his was one way he could influence them to adopt, as he had, the culture of heaven. Being a living visual aid of a heavenly life was an important aspect of his disciple-making.

But that was Paul, a singular figure in church history. Does this apply to church leaders today?

Yes.

I know this might not seem fair. Some will protest, "But we live in a different world." Actually we don't. We live in the same world. Same rock orbiting the same star. Satan is the same. Jesus is the same. Our sins are the same. Our redeemer is the same. Our mission is the same. Making disciples means the same thing now that it meant then.

There isn't any reason to think Paul's instruction to imitate him wasn't meant to be generalized to all believers in all cultures, so it must be possible to imitate Paul everywhere. It could be that your church's leaders have prayerfully concluded that God wants them to imitate Paul in their own country rather than in places with demon-infested slave girls. If so, then the persecution that arises from their imitation of Paul may take a different form than did Paul's in Philippi. So be it. We're simply called to imitate Godly examples, not to provoke any particular response. What form of persecution our imitation prompts depends on the earth culture in which we minister. But as we discussed earlier, we can be certain that all who follow Jesus will suffer for doing so. Churches need leaders who testify with their lives that following Jesus is worth this suffering. Churches need to see their leaders suffer for their faith, and then faithfully respond. There may be no surer way to end the influence of earth culture on our churches.

> You [Timothy], however, have followed my [Paul's] teaching, my conduct, my aim in life, my faith, my patience, my love, my steadfastness, *my persecutions and sufferings* that happened to me at Antioch, at Iconium, and at Lystra – which persecutions I endured; yet from them all the Lord rescued me. Indeed, *all who desire to live a godly life in Christ Jesus will be persecuted*, while evil people and impostors will go on from bad to worse deceiving and being deceived.
>
> II Tim 3:10-13

Paul used his persecution to influence and inspire Timothy. Clearly Paul understood that imitating him would unavoidably involve enduring the consequent persecution. Today's leaders must also use their example of enduring persecution to influence the Timothys in their churches. All of us need real-life examples so that we can be prepared to endure the suffering necessary to bring the gospel everywhere.

> You know what kind of men we proved to be among you for your sake. And you became imitators of us and of the Lord, for you received the word in much affliction, with the joy of the Holy Spirit, so that you became an example to all the believers in Macedonia and Achaia.
>
> I Thes 1:5b-7

> Remember your leaders, those who spoke to you the word of God. Consider the outcome of their way of life, and imitate their faith.
>
> Hebrews 13:7

Imitating imitation-worthy leaders wasn't a concept just for the early church. It is an enduring discipleship principle. Look at the next sentence in this passage.

> Jesus Christ is the same yesterday and today and forever.
>
> Hebrews 13:8

Who can live like Paul lived? Perhaps not many. But then, James warns that not many of us should be teachers. Spiritual teaching is more than transferring information. It is an invitation to examine and imitate the teacher's life. God wants teachers willing to serve as imitated examples. Is this happening in your church?

How does your church select its leaders?

If your church doesn't use imitation of Paul as a criterion for choosing leaders, how does it choose them? What common characteristics do you find in your leadership? Sadly, many churches choose leaders like worldly organizations choose leaders. Beyond academic credentials, they want men who know how to balance budgets, manage people and projects, increase market share, and/or sell a product. They want men who have shown they have what it takes to "succeed" in the world. But scripture doesn't mention worldly "success" as a criterion for church leadership. In fact, James' letter warns us against showing partiality to the "successful" among us. The partiality of which James warns isn't only about who sits on the floor, it's also about who sits in the "good place" of church authority!

> My brothers, show no partiality as you
> hold the faith in our Lord Jesus Christ,
> the Lord of glory. For if a man wearing a
> gold ring and fine clothing comes into
> your assembly, and a poor man in
> shabby clothing also comes in, and if

you pay attention to the one who wears the fine clothing and say, "You sit here in a good place," while you say to the poor man, "You stand over there," or, "Sit down at my feet," have you not then made distinctions among yourselves and become judges with evil thoughts? Listen, my beloved brothers, has not God chosen those who are poor in the world to be rich in faith and heirs in the kingdom, which he has promised to those who love him? But you have dishonored the poor man.

Jas 2:1-6a

Few churches seek the wisdom of poor men in shabby clothes. Maybe that is because few churches think such men have any wisdom.

I hope your church did well on this quiz. If it did, I guess you can stop here. But if not, *please* keep reading!

6
WHAT CAN YOU DO?

If your church didn't score well on the quiz, don't despair. That won't help the kingdom! Instead, begin earnestly living heaven culture! You can count on God's blessing. After all, this is more important to him than it ever can be to you! Let's talk first about seeking heaven culture individually, then about seeking it collectively.

To best help your church, you must first start where you have the most influence, with yourself. Imitate Christ. Ask him to show you how to imitate him better. Strive in every way to know him. Church attendance, devotional Bible readings, and prayers before meals won't be enough. Remind yourself constantly of the price he paid for you. Become a student of history. Learn something of the immense human suffering that took place over centuries so that the gospel could come to you. Learn about the sacrifice involved in producing the first English Bibles. Immerse yourself in Jesus, his word, and his culture.

If you want to be a godly influence in your church, the culture of heaven can't be a side interest that you fit around your "real world" schedule. The pursuit of heaven's culture must *become* your real world! If there is an aspect of your life that doesn't fit in this new context, you'll need to deal with that some way as soon as possible. God will show you how and he will make you able. This struggle won't be quick or easy. It will last the rest of your life and it will be harder than anything anyone has ever asked of you.

Listen to Paul:

> But whatever gain I had I count as loss for the sake of Christ. Indeed, I count everything as loss because of the surpassing worth of knowing Christ Jesus my Lord. For his sake I have suffered the loss of all things and count them as rubbish, in order that I may gain Christ and be found in him, not having a righteousness of my own that comes from the law, but that which comes through faith in Christ, the righteousness from God that depends on faith – that I may know him and the power of his resurrection, and may share in his sufferings, becoming like

him in his death, that by any means possible I may attain the resurrection from the dead. Not that I have already obtained this or am already perfect, but I press on to make it my own, because Christ Jesus has made me his own. Brothers, I do not consider that I have made it my own. But one thing I do: forgetting what lies behind and *straining forward* to what lies ahead, I *press on* toward the goal for the prize of the upward call of God in Christ Jesus. Let those of us who are mature think this way, and if in anything you think otherwise, God will reveal that also to you.

Phil 3:7-15

Did you hear the muscular language Paul uses? Straining forward. Pressing on. I have a son and daughter who are Marines. Ask them for stories of boot camp and you'll hear a lot about straining forward and pressing on. Becoming a Marine isn't easy! Neither is becoming an imitator of Christ. It's hard, intense work! Paul had rejected a religion of cultural self-justification. Paul was seeking Jesus. Imitate men like him who are *straining forward, pressing on* to imitate Christ. Beware of casual imitators. Imitation of Jesus isn't casual.

Second, imitate Jesus' love for his bride, the church. Individual imitation of Christ is not enough. Jesus loves his church, and he wants her holy. It's impossible to love Jesus and be ambivalent about his bride. The description of him and his church in the last 9 verses of Ephesians 5 is almost embarrassingly passionate. He is washing her, cleaning away every spot and blemish in order to someday present her to himself sanctified, her cleansing finally complete. On that day, she will literally embody the culture of heaven.

The more fervent your imitation of Jesus, the more zealous you will become for the holiness of his church. Don't expect everyone to share your zeal or even understand it. Just know that Jesus shares it, and learn to let that be enough.

This concern can be burdensome. To a long list of extreme sufferings he'd endured for the sake of the gospel, Paul added this one:

> And apart from all other things, there is the daily pressure on me of my anxiety for all the churches. Who is weak, and I am not weak? Who is made to fall, and I am not indignant?
>
> II Cor 11:28-29

The bride's cleansing is by no means complete. There remain many blemishes, many aspects of her thoughts and aspirations that aren't heavenly. Every one of these blemishes has at its core some vestige of earth culture. What does Jesus expect of us when we discover one?

Our response depends on our position in the church.

For Leaders

If you are a leader, remember this. Someday you will stand before Jesus and give an account for the condition of the souls you were charged to over-watch.

> Obey your leaders and submit to them, for they are keeping watch over your souls, as those who will have to give an account.
>
> Hebrews 13:17

He might ask you about the building or the budget or your church's mission statement, but I doubt it. Scripture suggests he'll keenly focus on how you shepherded his sheep. Your job isn't to keep them in the pen another week. You're a shepherd. Your job is to take the sheep somewhere. To foster their shift in identity from citizens of earth to citizens of heaven, to help them become members of Christ's functioning body, living stones being built into one spiritual house, one holy priesthood offering themselves as living sacrifices, and ready for whatever unholy response arises from the nonbelieving world.

You are tasked with leading them away from living earth culture and showing them how to live heaven culture. Your duty as leader is to equip them for ministry (Eph 4:11-12), so that your church can take its place in finishing the final preparations for Jesus' return.

He expects you to do it zealously (Rom 12:8), joyfully (Heb 13:18), and sacrificially (John 10:11), so that in everything pertaining to your church, God is glorified through Jesus Christ.

Remember, if God's desire was for his sheep to stay put, he would have given them fences. Instead, he gave them shepherds. Where are you taking the sheep he placed under your care? If you can't answer this question, chances are good you're not taking them anywhere. You're fine with earth-culture sheep as long as they stay in the pen.

But God isn't fine with that. And they're *his* sheep! Take them where he wants them to be.

You must also understand some of your fellow leaders may have earthly motives. It's always been like that. Being zealous for the purity of God's church means you must confront such men and expose these motives when necessary. It probably won't be fun.

In his final address to the elders of the church at Ephesus, Paul warns:

> Pay careful attention to yourselves and to all the flock, in which the Holy Spirit has made you overseers, to care for the church of God, which he obtained with his own blood. I know that after my departure fierce wolves will come in among you, not sparing the flock, and

> *from your own selves* will arise men speaking twisted things, to draw away the disciples after them.
>
> Acts 20:28-30

This wasn't merely a theoretical concern for Paul, and it must not be for leaders today.

> As I [Paul] urged you [Timothy] when I was going to Macedonia, remain at Ephesus so that you may charge certain persons not to teach any different doctrine...
>
> I Tim 1:3

Recent evangelical tendency has been to try to compel nonbelievers to live like believers by influencing our government, while simultaneously ignoring our responsibility to expect believers to live like Christ by influencing our church. It's a strange phenomenon.

Modern American evangelicalism has spent great energy to engineer legislation to compel those outside the church to behave as though they were Christian. Hence the emphasis on political alliances, legislative influence, Supreme Court nominations, etc. But these are earth culture means to achieve earth culture ends. Christ never told us to use secular institutions to compel nonbelievers to act like believers. He came to bring people to heaven, not to a "Christian" U.S. The only strategy by which God wants the church to influence the world is to proclaim the gospel while living the culture of heaven. That's how our ancient brothers turned their world upside down. We would do well to see Jesus' church, not our government, as our main focus.

As we have become more focused on using our earthly government to influence the behavior of those outside the church, we have all but neglected our clear scriptural responsibility to teach and expect heaven culture within the church. In I Corinthians 5, Paul instructed the church to remove a certain brother from fellowship. He gave two reasons. First, he expressed hope that this would prompt soul-saving repentance on the part of the brother. But he also wanted the church to not be "leavened" by the brother's sin, i.e. he did not want this earth culture contaminant to become established in the church.

> For what have I to do with judging outsiders? Is it not those inside the church whom you are to judge? God judges those outside. Purge the evil person from among you.
>
> I Cor 5:12-13

Has your church "purged" anyone recently? If not, why not? Is it because there is no evil person among you? Maybe it is because church membership has become so vague that it isn't even clear who is inside and who is outside. Or maybe it is because your leaders are more afraid of blowback from purging evil people than they are of evil leavening. This is really hard! Too hard for earth culture-inspired leadership!

Leaders, you must also nurture within your church a climate of yearning for congregation-specific divine instruction. The leaders of the church at Antioch understood they needed more than general revelation, they needed to know what God had in mind for them. It was in a season of intense, intentional spiritual focus that they received exactly that from God in Acts 13. In this expectant atmosphere, God's directive was so clearly discerned that they needed no time for discussion, took no time for planning, but obeyed immediately. Such an atmosphere doesn't just happen. No financial allocation can create it. This takes spiritual leadership.

> Now there were in the church at Antioch prophets and teachers, Barnabas, Simeon who was called Niger, Lucius of Cyrene, Manaen a lifelong friend of Herod the tetrarch, and Saul. While they were worshipping the Lord and fasting, the Holy Spirit said, 'Set apart for me Barnabas and Saul for the work to which I have called them.' Then after fasting and praying they laid their hands on them and sent them off.
>
> Acts 13:1-3

Finally, you must ready your church to do humanly impossible ministry. Leader, take a minute to think of the various ministries of your church. Suppose you have a visitor come from an out-of-town church. They've heard about your church and they want to see for themselves. Suppose you are the one chosen to show them around.

What ministry would you show them first? Would you explain how well you had planned it, how well your church had gathered and allocated resources, how well you had budgeted the anticipated staff time, how well you were monitoring progress toward goals, how well you had arranged accountability, how well you had ensured that it wouldn't go beyond the boundaries of investment you'd set for it? In short, would you show them how your church was making this ministry happen? And how would they respond? Maybe something like "Wow! I'm impressed! You guys are doing a great work here!"

Maybe you don't need to imagine. Maybe that very thing is happening in your church right now. If so, you've got a problem. That's *not* what God wants from us. He wants people to see our good works and give glory to *him,* not to us. But that can't happen if we insist on using earth culture thinking to do ministry. When we do, any ascribed glory goes toward us.

We can't let the fact that some may admire us for such ministry serve to affirm it in our minds. God warns us not to be intoxicated by human admiration. He is looking for disciples willing do ministry only he directs, only he supports, only he affirms, only he enables, and which glorifies only him.

How, then, is ministry supposed to happen? How does heaven culture-based ministry look? Its characteristic attribute is that it transcends earth culture. It demands more than human organizational skills, human resources, human *anything* can provide. Ministry taking place in a heaven culture context necessarily glorifies God because it is ministry that couldn't happen without him.

The church cannot see itself as a Christian version of the Rotary club. Here's what I mean. Rotary International introduces itself on its website this way:

"Rotary is a global network of 1.2 million neighbors, friends, leaders, and problem-solvers who see a world where people unite and take action to create lasting change – across the globe, in our communities, and in ourselves."

Sounds something like the church doesn't it? A global network uniting people to create lasting change in individuals and communities everywhere. I like the Rotary club very much. They do beautiful work. I hope they continue to do so. Bringing human resources together to help people is *very* good. But that's not why God made the church.

We can't function like a Christian Rotary club if we hope to fulfill the mandate God gave us. Our good works must not be explainable in human terms. We must discern God calling us to works we cannot do, and then obey him anyway, relying only on his provision. We must obey beyond the limits of self-sufficiency, even collective self-sufficiency. We must set aside our fear of appearing foolish, counting God's approval sufficient. That's the culture of heaven. Those are the good works he wants from us. Those are the good works that result in *his* glory, the works that distinguish God's church from every institution inspired by human goodwill and powered by human resources.

Does your church have ministries like *that*? Do you have ministries that couldn't exist without Jesus' guidance, the Holy Spirit's power, and the Father's resources? Do you have good works that you can't claim, works in which your church's only input was simply imprudent, prayerful obedience? Are people coming to ask about *them*? If so, wonderful! Invite me too! I also want to come and see and glorify God with you!

But if you don't have ministries like that, you've got a culture problem. Ask God to use you to transform your church. He's ready and able.

For "Non-Leaders"

Not a leader? Not in a position of authority? You still have influence, and God expects you to use every bit of it to help your church change. Read the letters to the seven churches in Revelation chapters 2 and 3. Please. I mean it. Stop and read them again.

In the letters to two of the churches, Jesus has nothing but praise. However, in the other five, Jesus expresses a major complaint. Each of these complaints is an example of some aspect of earth culture having become incorporated into the church. There were significant lapses in leadership here, and Jesus' criticism is graphic. Even in these churches, however, there were some still faithful to Jesus. Membership in such a sick church must have been a miserable experience for those members. But in each letter, there exists an expression of hope. Jesus makes a promise in each case to "the one who conquers." There is no indication this promise was only meant for leaders. This is important! We all have influence, and we are all expected to use our influence to conquer. And what is to be the focus of this conquering? The earth culture in our churches. Yikes!

Jesus could have told the remaining faithful to just move on and find a healthier church. After all, the church at Sardis was described as spiritually dead! That's not a human criticism, it is Jesus' divine assessment. Surely God wouldn't want people to stay in a spiritually dead church would he? Actually yes, it seems he does. Even in Sardis, he encourages the faithful to conquer. And leaving rarely leads to conquering. The implication is that Jesus expects every one of us to love his church so much that we will do the hard work of conquering whatever is standing between what our church is and what God wants it to be.

Don't miss this, reader. The earth-culture response to unholiness in a church is to leave and look for a holier church. But the heaven-culture response is to stay and conquer. The best way to ensure you'll never conquer anything is to leave. Remember, we're not religious consumers, we're living sacrifices. Again, no New Testament writer ever suggests anyone leave their church to seek a healthier one, despite major problems in many New Testament churches.

Ironically, one reason many people leave rather than conquer is that their church taught them to do so. Here's what I mean. If my present church used shiny programming to entice me away from another church, why wouldn't I leave if something even shinier shows up across town? Earth culture influence on the church never gets conquered if we teach people to *seek* a better church instead of *make* a better church.

[You may have noticed that even in the letters to the two healthy churches, people were also expected to conquer. Fact is, Jesus wants all of us to be conquerors. If our church is healthy, we'll be able to focus on conquering Satan's influence on people *outside* the church. If our church is unhealthy, we'll need to spend at least some of our energy conquering Satan's influence on people *inside* the church. Either way, Jesus expects his people to conquer Satan's influence.]

So staying is important. But it's not enough. We're supposed to conquer, remember? But conquering sounds like hurting people and blowing things up. Is that what God has in mind? No. His kind of conquering is much harder.

> For though we walk in the flesh, we are not waging war according to the flesh. For the weapons of our warfare are not of the flesh but have divine power to destroy strongholds.
>
> II Cor 10:3-4

Here's what heaven culture conquering looks like for those of us with influence but no authority as recognized leaders:

Pray. Pray for specific changes you believe God wants to see in your church. Pray with other believers. Be careful that you are praying *for* your church, not *against* it. Pray against Satan's influence. Don't pray against people. Be sure your prayers are not self-serving. Pray hard. And don't stop praying!

Some people in my church have been meeting for years to pray that God will change our congregation in the following eight specific ways.

1. May he break us with the truth that people dying without Jesus will spend eternity in hell.
2. May he make us understand that in Jesus we are all priests.

3. May he make us hungry for news about the advancing kingdom, and the task yet remaining.
4. May he make us eager to offer everything we own, even our very lives, in his service.
5. May he send 10% of us to the advancing edges of his kingdom by 2028.
6. May he inspire the 90% who stay to sacrificially send the 10% who sacrificially go.
7. May he show us how to embrace the Christians from other cultures living in our town.
8. May he bring our entire congregation to pray these prayers.

Submit. Pray for your leaders and submit to their leadership. Don't subvert their authority. If they are poor leaders, pray that they will become better leaders. For all you know, God may have decided he will teach them how to lead well *only after* he has taught you how to submit to them and obey them well. You have no right to insist he do it the other way around.

One way to ensure leaders will never become good leaders is to refuse to submit to their developing leadership. If they need to be challenged, scripture outlines a clear procedure in I Tim 5:19-21. This procedure doesn't involve gossip or insubordination. Remember, you're not mounting an insurrection, you're catalyzing a cultural revolution. Pray that your leaders will lead it!

Mentor someone. If you can inspire even one person to better live the culture of heaven, you've changed your church. If your church is like many, most members cannot identify anyone who is mentoring their spiritual growth. Mentoring isn't only for people like Paul. Anyone can mentor. Simply reading God's word with someone can be astonishingly powerful. You may be surprised to learn how many members of your church don't have even a basic knowledge of the Bible. Perhaps you are one of them.

If you've never had a mentor, you might not know how to mentor. That's OK. God will teach you. Ask God to show you how to help someone move forward in their imitation of Christ. Again, don't try to work this in around the margins of your life. Let this become central in your life. This is an investment in God's church, and is therefore worthy of great sacrifice.

Live an imitated life. Again, this isn't only for leaders. In fact, if you do this *you will be a leader* whether your church leadership recognizes you as one or not. Most of us have been taught in church that the humble person eschews imitation. But that is earth culture humility. One aspect of our imitation of Christ is living a life which invites imitation, just like he did. True, the world shows us prideful people inviting imitation for earthly reasons. But scripture shows us humble people inviting imitation for heavenly reasons. Every believer can and should live a life which is being imitated. One way Paul invited imitation was by inviting others to come alongside him in ministry. You can do that too. It's part of following Jesus' example.

Be tenacious. I know of no scriptural promise that the church changes you desire will come quickly. Your efforts may not bear visible fruit for decades. They may not have effect until after you've passed from this life. Can you be faithful to "pray without ceasing" for God's church despite seeing nothing change? Or do you believe you must see results to validate your efforts? Remember, you don't even know how to evaluate what you are seeing. If God's Holy Spirit within you validates your efforts, persevere in them!

Be strong. There isn't any reason to expect this to be easy. Expect opposition, mainly from earth culture strongholds within your church. Some of the greatest reformers in the history of the church have endured severe opposition, even martyrdom, at the hands of their own churches. Do you love God's church enough to suffer *at its hands* for its benefit? God has empowered many before you to suffer for his bride, and he is ready to empower you as well.

These are the weapons of our warfare. This is how we conquer.

Let's pause for a minute. We have just discussed some hard teachings. I'm afraid I may have left some of you thinking that living the culture of heaven is a joyless and grim endeavor. That would be a great injustice, for there is *great* joy in living heaven culture. It is, however, joy that those living earth culture simply cannot know.

We can read much about how Jesus, Paul, and others suffered when living heaven culture brought them into conflict with their earth cultures. But we can also read of the joy they experienced for the very same reason. Consider these scriptures:

> ...and when they had called in the apostles, they beat them and charged them not to speak in the name of Jesus, and let them go. Then they left the presence of the council, rejoicing that they were counted worthy to suffer dishonor for the name.
>
> Acts 5:40-41

> Even if I am to be poured out as a drink offering upon the sacrificial offering of your faith, I am glad and rejoice with you all. Likewise you also should be glad and rejoice with me.
>
> Phil 2:17-18

> And you became imitators of us and of the Lord, for you received the word in much affliction, with the joy of the Holy Spirit...
>
> I Thes 1:6

> ...looking to Jesus, the founder and perfecter of our faith, who for the joy that was set before him endured the cross, despising the shame, and is seated at the right hand of the throne of God.
>
> Heb 12:2

When we can rejoice to be counted worthy of suffering for the name, when we can joyfully accept that our life is being poured out for the advancement of God's kingdom rather than for our "success," when we can endure *anything* by focusing on the joy Jesus has set before us, then we will be living the culture of heaven. We will have rejected the world's definition of a blessed life in favor of Jesus' definition. And we will know fellowship with every follower everywhere all through the ages who has known the same joy.

Are there joys in earth culture? Of course! But even the best and noblest of these joys will fade. The joy that is peculiar to heaven culture will last forever.

Let me illustrate with a true story. As I mentioned, I work for a faith-based nonprofit which helps our local churches welcome refugees. Jesus expects this of his people. It is one of the ways he has chosen for us to demonstrate his heart to the world. But the earth culture in us often protests.

Ken (not his real name) loved Jesus, but he wasn't sure how he felt about refugees coming to our town. Despite my best efforts, our discussions about refugees generally ended up being about US national security. Ken couldn't think about refugees in the context of heaven culture, only in the context of his earth culture. He was afraid that refugees coming to our country, especially to our town, would somehow compromise his lifestyle and he didn't want that. I watched God change that one day. It took about four hours.

Through the nonprofit, Ken's small group had agreed to welcome San (not his real name), a refugee from Burma. Part of welcoming San involved meeting him at the airport. But on the night of San's arrival Ken was exhausted from a long day at work, and the airport pickup was scheduled for 11:30 PM at an airport about an hour's drive away. Ken tried to excuse himself, but his group leader convinced him to come along anyway. He finally agreed, but with considerable reluctance.

They got to the airport only to learn that the plane was delayed. What would have been a long night dragged on into a *very* long night. Small talk eventually gave way to naps in uncomfortable chairs. But then the magic happened. The plane arrived and Ken met San. What had been a politically-charged idea was instantly transformed into a person bearing God's image.

Until that night, Ken couldn't have found Burma on a map. He didn't know people were fleeing that country, why they were fleeing, or where they were going. He didn't know because he didn't care. He didn't care because he couldn't see how it affected him. In his earth culture thinking, their problems didn't affect him as long as they stayed wherever they were, somewhere far away. So why care?

But that night it began to matter to Ken that San comes from an ethnic group still unreached by the gospel of Christ, a group without a single word of scripture translated into their language. Now it matters to Ken that another unreached, scripture-less people has driven San's people out of Burma to a refugee camp in Bangladesh. Now Ken knows San, a real person from one of the spiritually darkest places on earth, a man who has a wife and three sons still living a perilous life in that camp. San knew only a little English, but Ken heard him say "My heart is sad" when talking about leaving his family.

On the drive back from the airport Ken was a different man. He wasn't talking politics or national security anymore. He was wondering aloud if Jesus might want to send someone to bring the gospel to the people in that camp. Ken loved Jesus before that night, but now he loves him differently. He *sees* him differently. Now he is beginning to see Jesus from the vantage point of heaven culture, the same way he now sees San. A life-long transformation has begun. His earth culture fear of losing his American way of life is being replaced by a heaven culture desire to increase God's glory.

In those four hours, Ken got a taste of the peculiar joy known only to those living the culture of heaven. And who knows? Maybe Jesus has in mind to send Ken to bring the gospel to that camp! Ken himself may one day be poured out like a drink offering on the sacrificial offering of San's faith and that of his family. If so, may they rejoice together in heaven forever!

Joy in the culture of heaven is joy no earth culture can understand.

7

THE PROBLEM WITH BUDGETS

Sorry church leaders, I'm not done with you yet. Let me ask you a question. What could your church do to advance God's kingdom if someone gave you all the resources you could possibly need? All the money, all the time, all the connections, all the expertise, all the *everything*! What would you do? What if your only limitation was the degree to which your congregation was willing to live the culture of heaven?

I have good news for you! That exact thing has already happened. Hear Jesus' words:

> "Fear not, little flock, for *it is your Father's good pleasure to give you the kingdom.*"
>
> Luke 12:32

> And he [Jesus] said to him [the elder
> brother of the prodigal son], "Son, you
> are always with me, *and all that is mine
> is yours*."

Luke 15:31

God has given his kingdom to us. That's not just an idea. That's everything there is. We didn't have to earn it, or take it, or deserve it. God gave it to us. Why? Because it pleased him to do so. Let that soak in a second. God is so pleased for believers in Jesus to live as citizens of his kingdom that he gives them everything.

This kingdom is unlike any earthly kingdom. This is the kingdom of our Father who owns everything. Every subject of this kingdom owns everything owned by the Father, which again, is everything. When God said he owns the cattle on a thousand hills, he wasn't talking about livestock. He was talking about *everything*. This is the kingdom of God. Think about this. God, unlike any earthly king, never has to decide how to allocate scarce resources, because there aren't any scarce resources in his kingdom.

So church leaders, if you find yourselves spending time discussing how to allocate limited resources, please hear this: that is earth culture thinking. Stop it. Live in the kingdom of God. Live the culture of heaven. God has been pleased to give his people everything they need to serve him. As long as we are with him, all that is his is ours. *All that is his is ours!* Live that truth!

I understand this sounds pie-in-the-sky impossible. "Obviously, James, you've never had to deal with real-world finance". Actually, I have. I spent years as a "successful" professional, running my own business, and living a "Christianized" version of earth culture. I'm trying to put that behind me now and you can too. Live heaven culture. Your church *needs* that from you.

This has always been difficult for us humans to believe, even those of us who know Jesus. Look at the context of Luke 12:32 above. Jesus was telling his disciples not to worry about food and clothing. Why? Because God feeds the birds and clothes the grass, and he likes us more than he likes them.

> "But if God so clothes the grass, which is alive in the field today, and tomorrow is thrown into the oven, how much more will he clothe you, O you of little faith? And do not seek what you are to eat and what you are to drink, nor be worried. For all the nations of the world seek after these things, and your Father knows that you need them. Instead seek his kingdom, and these things will be added to you. Fear not, little flock, for it is the Father's good pleasure to give you the kingdom. Sell your possessions, and give to the needy. Provide yourselves with moneybags that do not grow old, with a treasure in

the heavens that does not fail, where no thief approaches and no moth destroys. For where your treasure is, there will your heart be also."

Luke 12:28-34

Did you catch the promises of unlimited resources? You can feel free to "imprudently" use up your resources in ministry knowing that God will provide anew from his limitless abundance. You can give so much away that you don't even have anything left to feed yourself. God won't think you're foolish. He'll think you're faithful. And then he'll feed you. That's a promise only we believers can claim.

But here's the kicker. Jesus isn't only telling us we *can* live like this. He's telling us we *must*. If we refuse, if we insist on being prudent by worldly standards, if we cannot bring ourselves to consider God's promise more real than things we can touch and count, if we believe our job is to allocate limited earthly resources, if we insist on holding something back so that we'll have enough for ourselves, we will certainly fail to show the world who God is and how he works. We must choose to keep our focus on the uncountable "treasure in the heavens that does not fail," rather than think our job is to wisely divide a fixed-size pie.

This bears repeating. Leaders, if you see your church's ministry as being limited by finite dollar amounts on a budget sheet, you are failing your church. If you haven't already, you will. You will allow human projections of church revenue to determine ministry. This is earth culture, not heaven culture. Jesus said you can't serve both God and money. I can't find anywhere in the Bible where God ever tells leaders of his people to balance a budget. The letters to the churches in Revelation don't mention budgets. Hebrews 13:17 doesn't say leaders will give account to God for budgets. They will instead give account for how well they watched over the souls entrusted to their care.

The possessors of these souls are watching your example now, leaders. If they see you approaching ministry with an earthly business-model worldview, they will as well. They also will set their finances as the final deciding factor regarding what they can or can't do in the kingdom of God. In doing so, they too will discount God's promise of unlimited resources. They will see countable earthly treasure as a more powerful determiner of their obedience than uncountable treasure in heaven. And their hearts will be bound to earth, not to heaven. Jesus said so.

And you, leader, will be called to account for that. Are you ready to present a balanced church budget as your defense?

I know this doesn't sound practical. That's not the issue, though, is it? God never promised to be practical, and he never told us to be practical either. Practical is earth culture. Instead, God is faithful. And he expects faithfulness from us. The culture of heaven is all about that. Let me give you a real life example.

A few years ago a church I know was beginning to discover they could send missionaries from among their own 2,000 member congregation. Their leaders came to believe they should create a full-time staff position to foster this sending, but they'd never had such a position before. There wasn't a budget line for this new position. So they were faced with a dilemma. On the one hand they believed God wanted them to create the position. On the other hand, it didn't fit their budget.

Here's what could have happened. The leadership could have called out to God with fasting and prayer, "Father we believe you are calling us to add this staff position but we have made a budget that doesn't allow it. What is your plan? What shall we do?"

They could have gone to the congregation and clearly laid out the dilemma. It could have been an occasion for a season of intense congregational prayer. This might have inspired congregational sacrifice to fund the position. They could have appealed to the rest of the staff to voluntarily lower their salaries to accommodate the new position. They could have set the budget aside and simply brought a mission minister on board anyway, trusting God to provide above the church's budgeted income until time to make another budget. Any of these pathways would have been an opportunity for God to show this congregation how he funds the ministry he commands. But none of these things happened.

Here's what did happen. Holding their budget as the final determiner of ministry, they withdrew enough funding from the missionaries they supported to accommodate the salary of the new staff position, so that the new position had no net effect on the budget. Don't miss the irony. These leaders relied on earthly financial reasoning to do work that made no earthly sense. If this church is ever to become a church after God's heart, it must learn to honor God's heart over its budget. There has never been an unfunded mandate in the history of God's kingdom. Remember, our Father owns everything. He expects us to act like we believe it.

Do you see the underlying culture problem? It's always the same thing, earth culture versus heaven culture. It's so easy for our earth culture to become so invisible to us that we don't realize how powerfully it shapes every decision we make. Leaders must resist the temptation to manage the household of God like businessmen manage businesses. God isn't impressed by churches who resolve to "live within their means." Consider the churches of Macedonia (this included the church at Philippi):

> We want you to know, brothers [in Corinth], about the grace of God that has been given among the churches of Macedonia, for in a severe test of

> affliction, their abundance of joy and
> their extreme poverty have overflowed
> in a wealth of generosity on their part.
> For they gave according to their means,
> as I can testify, *and beyond their means*,
> of their own accord, begging us
> earnestly for the favor of taking part in
> the relief of the saints...
>
> II Corinthians 8:1-4

Actually, I can't find any evidence in scripture of any church or any person ever getting into trouble for investing more in God's kingdom than God intended they invest. Can you? Instead I see Paul applauding the Macedonian churches for giving beyond their means, I see Jesus applauding the woman in the temple who gave all she had to live on.

God counts money differently than we do. Notice Jesus didn't say the widow's offering meant more to him, or warmed his heart more, or was more significant in some vague way. No. He said she gave *more*. *She gave more! Her gift was MORE!* What the world sees as reckless imprudence looks like reckless faithfulness to God. And he likes it. That's the big offering in his eyes.

What would it be like to be in a church where we lived as if we'd inherited *everything* and could obey without funding limitations? Where we didn't have to be careful to balance budgets we create? Where we could engage the ministry God sets before us and prayerfully leave the funding to him? Where the only factors determining ministry are "What is God telling us to do?" and "Are we willing to do it?"

What would it be like? I don't know either. But I want to know. I believe God wants all of us to know.

Have you ever had a believer excuse himself or his church from obeying Jesus in the guise of "counting the cost?" Here's how it works. We like to think we're obedient in ministry, but we also like to be in control of our obedience. We want to know in advance how much it will cost in time and money. So when Jesus sets before us ministry wherein the demands seem too open-ended, we look for a way out before we even get in.

"Counting the cost" is a common way for Biblically literate people to excuse themselves. They try to predict how much a particular ministry will cost. Then they look at how much they have. If they see the predicted cost as too high relative to what they have, they think they can excuse themselves with their spiritual reputation intact by saying they're merely following Jesus' command to "count the cost." But that kind of thinking is earth culture. Nothing more than prudent, human-centered earth culture.

This isn't what Jesus was teaching in this passage, Luke 14:28-33. In fact, it is the exact opposite. He wasn't advising that we demand God detail the cost before we obey so that we can decide if we're interested or not. That's not counting the cost. That's disobedience.

Instead, in this passage Jesus taught that we must decide in advance that following Jesus is worth even undetermined cost. Up to and including everything. Period. Jesus never tells anyone how much their obedience will cost or how long it will take except to say it will cost everything and take forever.

That's the cost of following Jesus. The cost of following Jesus is to not know all the details in advance. If we're not willing to pay *that* cost, we'll only do ministry that we can predict and afford and handle on our own. Of course, it's impossible to follow Jesus that way. So we must not "count the cost" like people in earth culture count cost. Instead we must discern what God would have us do, be sure we're ready to risk everything we've got (our money, our time, our reputations, our careers, our lives, our families' lives, *everything!*), then do it.

Read how Jesus ends this discussion of counting the cost. This is cost analysis in the culture of heaven.

> "So therefore, any one of you who does not renounce all that he has cannot be my disciple."
>
> Luke 14:33

Jesus always advertised the cost of discipleship the same way. It costs everything. But it's always worth it. I'll say it once again; Jesus wants us to assume every act of obedience will cost us everything, then obey anyway. That's heaven culture.

If the church at Antioch evaluated prospective ministry like many of our churches do, they might *still* be "counting the cost," trying to decide if they could afford to send Saul and Barnabas or not. My guess is that Saul and Barnabas would have eventually been sent; just by a different church. If your church insists on earth culture cost-counting, God may use a different church to send your Paul and Barnabas as well, while you're working on your budget.

Please don't misunderstand. Scripture does not condone wastefulness. And God doesn't promise to rescue us from being lazy. He does, however, promise to bless us so that we have the means to be obedient in ministry. We absolutely can decide to obey without arranging the finances in advance.

> Each one must give as he has decided in his heart, not reluctantly or under compulsion, for God loves a cheerful giver. And God is able to make all grace abound to you, *so that having all sufficiency in all things at all times, you may abound in every good work*.
>
> II Cor 9:8

> He who supplies seed to the sower and bread for food will supply and multiply

your seed for sowing and increase the harvest of your righteousness. *You will be enriched in every way to be generous in every way*, which through us will produce thanksgiving to God.

II Cor 9:10-11

You've heard Philippians 4:19 quoted many times, "And my God will supply every need of yours according to his riches in glory in Christ Jesus." Maybe you've even sung it. It's true, but don't miss the context. Here's the whole passage:

> Yet it was kind of you [the Philippian church] to share my trouble. And you Philippians yourselves know, that in the beginnings of the gospel, when I left Macedonia, no church entered into partnership with me in giving and receiving, except you only. Even in Thessalonica you sent me help for my needs once and again. Not that I seek the gift, but I seek the fruit that increases to your credit. I have received full payment, and more. I am well supplied, having received from Epaphroditus the gifts you sent, a fragrant offering, a sacrifice acceptable and pleasing to God. And my God will supply every need of yours according to his riches in glory in Christ Jesus. To our

God and Father be glory forever and
ever. Amen.

Phil 4:14-20

So much here! It seems as though Paul's apostolic band
had left Antioch on his second missionary trip without
sufficient financial support to take them any further
than Philippi. Through much suffering, Paul and Silas
planted a church there. Now, with only this newborn
Philippian church supporting him, Paul's group
continued on to Thessalonica, which was *not* on the
way back to Antioch, by the way! He was in
Thessalonica no more than three weeks, but the
Philippian church sent him support "once and again"
while he was there!

Don't miss this. The Philippians had seen Paul obey God
beyond the limits of financial prudence, so they did as
well. No wonder this church was commended
elsewhere by Paul for giving beyond their means. Why
were they imprudently generous? They were simply
imitating Paul's imprudent obedience! Years later, they
were still sacrificially supporting him in his ministry.
That's why Paul was confident God would supply every
need of theirs according to his riches in glory. If we
want the same assurance, we would do well to follow
their example. Don't let budgets determine ministry. Let
God's Holy Spirit determine ministry. Then obey,
trusting his provision will follow your obedience.
Faithful people have been doing that for a long time.

8

A TALE OF TWO CHURCHES

This next part is also mainly meant for church leaders, but if you're still reading this you'll likely be a church leader someday! The book of Acts contains a wonderful leadership case study by vividly contrasting two churches, Jerusalem and Antioch. We looked at these two churches earlier but let's look again, paying particular attention to church leadership. Don't get lost in the weeds here. It will all make sense in the end.

This time, let's focus on how the leaders in these two churches managed (or mismanaged) the adoption by their churches of the culture of heaven. Spoiler alert: Antioch handled it well, Jerusalem not so well. Antioch was sacrificially invested in kingdom growth, understood God has no favorite earth culture, and eventually became the kingdom's "operations center." Jerusalem, on the other hand, seemed reluctant to challenge ungodly vestiges of earth culture, was suspicious of heaven culture, and eventually became sidelined. Crucial leadership decisions made the difference.

Let's look at Antioch first. Most importantly, the leaders at Antioch weren't afraid of the culture of heaven. From its infancy, the leaders there seem to have perceived the "big thing" God was doing in their age, opening the kingdom to Gentiles. At a time when the church in Jerusalem thought a heterogeneous congregation meant Hebrew Jews mixing with Hellenist Jews, the church at Antioch was already preaching to Gentiles! Acts 11 tells us that the church at Antioch was born when Jewish Christians (including some from places as distant from Jerusalem as Africa) came preaching the gospel not only to Jews but to Greeks (Gentiles) as well.

The church at Antioch may have been the first Gentile/Jewish church to exist anywhere in the world, proving as never before that God intended to unite disparate peoples through the gospel of Jesus and engage all of them in his kingdom.

They surely knew that bringing Jews and Gentiles together in Antioch would drive certain elements of the Jerusalem church crazy. But hadn't Jesus taught that following him would offend people, especially religious people? So they did the right thing anyway. Antioch's wise leadership allowed God to build the church around the task of uniting people from different cultures under Christ to advance his gospel on the earth.

The church at Antioch was very generous. For example, consider the money the Antioch church sent to the church at Jerusalem in response to the famine in Acts 11:27-30. We know there were people in the church at Jerusalem that didn't even accept the Gentile believers at Antioch as brothers (read Acts 15:5), yet the Antioch church sent relief money to Jerusalem during the famine anyway, even though there is no record of them having been asked. Generosity like that doesn't stem from earth culture, only heaven culture. But as crazy as that was, it wasn't the craziest way they gave.

They sacrificially gave their people as well. The Antioch church was generous with its money, but even more generous with its people. In the beginning of chapter 13 there is a list of five leading prophets and teachers in the Antioch church. Two of those five were Saul (later known as Paul) and Barnabas, who had been there at least a year teaching "great numbers of people (11:26)" and who'd been entrusted by the Antioch church to take the relief money mentioned above to the church at Jerusalem. It would seem that in the eyes of the Antioch church, Saul and Barnabas were central figures.

But look what happened later in the same paragraph when the Holy Spirit indicated they were to be sent off to parts unknown on a rather vaguely defined "work". There is no discussion among the leadership as to how this will affect the congregation. Instead the leaders fasted, prayed, and sent them off. They didn't just leave, they were *sent*. Huge difference.

This is truly extraordinary. I've seen churches send people away to do kingdom work, but I've never personally seen a church send away a central figure, one of the main people. It tells me something about the Antioch congregation that they *sent* Paul and Barnabas. They understood that following Jesus necessarily involves not just personal sacrifice, but also congregational sacrifice.

The culture of heaven helps us see our congregations in the bigger context of God's growing kingdom. It helps us choose to sacrifice the talent we think our congregation needs for the greater needs of our global commission. Lots of churches send money they think they can spare. But that's not enough. God expects churches to send *people* they think they *can't* spare. Earth church culture says don't trade your "bread and butter" players. Heaven church culture says God decides who goes.

There are two reasons we must become more generous regarding people. First, people are the real currency of kingdom building. Churches ready to participate in building God's kingdom *must* focus on sending people.

Fundraising is fine, but it can never substitute for people-raising.

There's another reason. Money can't come back to the congregation to bear witness to divine activity out on the kingdom's edge. God knows only people can do that. Churches that only send money typically have little appreciation of what God is doing in our age to fulfill the promises he made long ago. They never hear the stories. Maybe you're wondering what I'm even talking about. If so, I feel sorry for you and for your church.

There are two other qualities of the Antioch church that are worth noting. The Antioch church, at least its leadership, was able to hear the voice of the Holy Spirit together. The first paragraph of chapter 13 describes a time of fasting and praying during which the voice of the Holy Spirit was heard. It isn't clear from the passage if the voice was heard by the group or relayed to the group by one of its members. No matter. There is no record of dispute within the group as to the authenticity of the message, despite the fact that it must have been surprising. They knew they'd heard from God.

Also, there seems to have been no hesitation in radical obedience on the part of the church. Given the context, there couldn't have been any doubt in anyone's mind this would be dangerous for the two sent out. This was a real sacrifice both for Saul and Barnabas and for the body at Antioch.

But all parties were willing to accept the risk because again, they were confident they'd heard from God!

Perhaps because of these qualities, the Antioch church served as a divine staging area for others who would soon be sent. In Acts chapters 11-15, God brings to Antioch four men he will later send out on mission: Barnabas, Saul, John Mark, and Silas. The first, Barnabas, is sent from Jerusalem to Antioch to investigate reports the Jerusalem church is hearing about the church at Antioch. Apparently he is excited by what he sees. Not only does he decide to remain in Antioch, but he goes to Tarsus to bring his old friend Saul to Antioch as well. Later, when Saul and Barnabas are sent to Jerusalem with the famine relief, they bring John Mark back to Antioch with them. Finally, in chapter 15, the letter containing the results of the council of Jerusalem was carried to Antioch by two men, one of whom is Silas, who stays in Antioch for a while before returning to Jerusalem. In the next paragraph, though, we see Silas back in Antioch, ready to go out with Paul on his second missionary journey!

Surely God had been preparing these men to be sent. Perhaps he saw Antioch as the only church ready to send them. It's difficult to imagine another reason for this migration of soon-to-be sent ones to Antioch. We read nothing to suggest any of them came to Antioch because they were disgruntled or disappointed with the state of affairs at Jerusalem or, in Saul's case, Tarsus.

They don't seem to have come to Antioch because of any earth-culture reasons. None of them came because of a job promotion, to retire near a beach, etc. There is no suggestion the Antioch church offered to better "meet their needs" by better preaching, better programming, etc. This seems to have been a Spirit-directed, kingdom-focused assembling of messengers of the gospel. It seems God was bringing heaven-culture people to a heaven-culture church.

The Antioch church, because its leaders were living the culture of heaven in sending Paul and Barnabas, was protected against earth culture-inspired attacks. The first paragraph of chapter 15 describes an attack on the Antioch church. Some men came from Judea and began teaching the necessity of keeping the law, including circumcision, as prerequisite to inclusion in God's kingdom. It is important to remember this wasn't an esoteric Bible-study topic then. Indeed, in a mixed Gentile/Jewish church it was an existential issue! Why then, does this earth culture-spawned attack seem to have caused no disturbance among the brothers in Antioch? Perhaps it is because of what had just happened verses before, in the final paragraph of chapter 14.

Paul and Barnabas had just returned from their journey, gathered the church together, and reported all that God had done through them. Antioch's perception that God was opening the doors of the kingdom to Gentiles was affirmed by Paul and Barnabas in story after story, fresh from the advancing edge of the kingdom. Imagine being there when Paul and Barnabas made their first, breathless reports… "Guys, we understood God's heart correctly. He *is* bringing the Gentiles into his kingdom, and not just here in Antioch – he is doing it everywhere we went!" What a powerful affirmation of correct theology!

And a timely one as well. When the would-be trouble-makers arrived from Jerusalem in the very next paragraph, they were treated almost as a nuisance rather than a threat. There is nothing in this passage to suggest Antioch sent Paul and Barnabas to Jerusalem so that the Antioch church could learn the truth. Antioch already knew the truth. Antioch sent Paul and Barnabas so that the *Jerusalem* church could know the truth.

That's why Paul and Barnabas didn't present a theological argument in Jerusalem. They simply reported everything God had done through them, including the signs and wonders God had done among the Gentiles. They countered Jerusalem's earth culture-informed theology with a simple and confident eye-witness report of what God was doing out on the edge.

Reports from the advancing edge of God's kingdom are essential. They affirm good theology and expose bad theology. The leadership in Antioch must be commended for making sure the entire church heard the report of the returnees. Global gospel ministry isn't just for "those who are interested in missions." Global gospel ministry is for everyone who follows Jesus. Healthy churches understand it is why the church was created. Leaders in such churches see that everyone hears breaking news of the advance of God's kingdom.

God neutralized the Judaizers' attack on the Antioch church first by sending Paul and Barnabas out and then bringing them home precisely when he did. The Antioch church received its ROKI (Return On Kingdom Investment) exactly when God knew they would need it most, just prior to a legalistic attack which might have otherwise been very damaging. Consequently, Antioch didn't stumble or even flinch when the attack occurred. There's no evidence of fearful paralysis or distraction from the mission.

They were confident enough to continue taking the gospel to Gentiles with or without the approval of the church at Jerusalem. This is evidenced by the fact that, though the Jerusalem Council did not directly address the issue of circumcision in their decree, the Antioch church didn't push for a "clear ruling," a direct once-and-for-all rebuttal of the circumcision party's central thesis. To do so might have taken much time and energy and become a disabling distraction.

The Antioch church had something more important to do, i.e. keep pushing the edge of the kingdom out toward the ends of the earth. In fact, in the paragraph immediately following the return of the council delegates, Antioch sent two teams out. The leaders in Antioch needed no affirmation but God's, no permission but God's, and no help but God's. They could not be discouraged, distracted, or stopped. They knew what God was doing and were set on playing their part in it.

Sadly, the account of the Jerusalem church reads very differently in this regard. While the Jerusalem church didn't miss every mark, it missed some badly. There are multiple occasions when church leadership avoided confronting that church's major impediment to engaging the kingdom, a belief that the earth culture of the majority of its members was God's favorite culture. They'd come to believe Jewish people were the only people God cared about. Leadership should have set itself to correcting this. But it didn't.

After a very Spirit-filled, Kingdom-minded beginning in the early chapters, leadership problems in the Jerusalem church soon become manifest. The controversy in chapter six regarding the disparity of food allocation between the Hebrew and Hellenist Jewish believers was "settled" by the choosing of the seven rather than by clear teaching from the apostles that God has no ethnic preference. Directly confronting the issues of culture and ethnicity then might have set a helpful precedent for the more problematic Jewish/Gentile issue soon to follow, but this opportunity to replace earth culture with heaven culture was missed. Instead, it seems that the leaders were more concerned with placating theologically errant believers than correcting them. Again, teaching heaven culture is hard, but "unteaching" earth culture is *very* hard! It upsets people. We don't know how God felt about the apostles' proposal to select the seven. The text doesn't tell us. We only know the people liked it. "This proposal pleased the whole gathering." (Acts 6:5)

Next, the dramatic bestowing of the Holy Spirit upon Samaritan believers in Acts chapter 8 was witnessed by both Peter and John, but there is no record of them returning to Jerusalem and presenting this truth and its implications to the church. A second opportunity to challenge the earth culture so strongly influencing their church seems to have been missed.

The apostles missed a third chance to decisively lead their congregation into heaven culture in Acts 10, when God sent Peter to Cornelius' house. They could have recognized this for what it was, a dramatic message from God not just for Peter but for the entire church, and proclaimed this critical "new" truth to the congregation.

But instead, Peter speaks only to the circumcision party, and only in response to their criticism. These circumcised believers had no further objections upon hearing him and to their credit, they glorified God. They correctly concluded that God had granted repentance "to the Gentiles also."

But here's the problem. There is no evidence that this conclusion or its implications were ever presented to the larger church. Sadly, subsequent events show instead that the significance of this milestone was apparently lost even to the ones who heard it, the circumcision party. How did church leadership not recognize this God-likes-us-best earth culture remnant as a central problem for their church?

That there was even need for a Council at Jerusalem in Chapter 15 confirms that the Gentile issue had not been settled in the Jerusalem church after Peter's experience with Cornelius. How much time had elapsed? It isn't clear from the text. Peter, however, speaking in Acts 15:7, refers to his experience with Cornelius in Acts 10 as taking place "in the early days." So it seems that God had given the Jerusalem leadership some time to introduce this cultural shift to their church. But there is no evidence they had done so.

The Council's eventual conclusion again suggests a leadership more interested in placation than in clarification. Peter had seen (and the leadership had previously acknowledged) uncircumcised Gentiles receiving the Holy Spirit and being baptized. A clear statement on circumcision is what the Jerusalem church needed from their leadership. Antioch didn't need it, Jerusalem did. But they didn't get it.

The final statement proposed by James in Acts 15:23-29 addressed circumcision only by inference. Again, subsequent events demonstrated that the statement did not adequately refute the earth culture theology in Jerusalem that needed to change. Both Jerusalem and Antioch accepted it. Perhaps that was the only goal of leadership. Unfortunately, the underlying problem remained unresolved.

Galatians 2:11-14 recounts a visit by Peter to Antioch. This visit seems to have been sometime after Peter's experience with Cornelius. During his visit Peter was eating with Gentile believers until "certain men came from James" (people from the circumcision party in the Jerusalem church) arrived in Antioch. At that point Peter withdrew from the Gentiles and was rebuked by Paul for doing so. Paul was recounting this event for the Gentile churches in Galatia at some later time. Why? Because the circumcision party was still around and had now come to trouble them too. Earth culture thinking in the Jerusalem church continued to pose problems for kingdom growth among the Gentile churches, and the problem wasn't limited to Antioch and the Galatian churches. Paul's letters to Rome, Corinth, Ephesus, Philippi, and Colossae dealt with it as well. Again, the primary source of this false teaching lay within the Jerusalem church. The leaders there knew it was happening and they knew it was wrong, but there is no record of them ever confronting these false teachers.

Years later, we see that they had allowed this false teaching to "leaven the whole loaf" of their church. When Paul presents himself to the Jerusalem church in 21:17, "the brothers" (apparently a group of leaders, not the entire church) received him warmly and listened to his report, but then straightaway warned him about the thousands of Jewish believers there, all of them "zealous for the law" and apparently either unaware of God's by-then-well-documented opening of his kingdom to Gentiles or unwilling to enjoin it. These Jewish believers had heard of Paul's work among the Gentiles but did not approve of it. "They will certainly hear that you have come" the leaders warned Paul, and he was advised to make a public display of his Jewishness through a temple ceremony to appease these immature believers, believers whose earth culture identity had been allowed to persist unchallenged for years.

So the Jerusalem church, which so badly needed to hear Paul's report of what God was doing on the edges of the Kingdom, heard nothing. Earth-culture informed theology persisted because leaders seem to have been more interested in maintaining a shallow illusion of harmony than in bringing their church to embrace heaven culture. One is reminded of the false prophets in Jeremiah 6:14 "They have healed the wound of my people lightly, saying 'Peace, peace,' when there is no peace." Sad for the Jerusalem church, but not a problem for God. He simply shifted his center of operations to Antioch.

Unchallenged bad theology insulated the Jerusalem church from the joy and excitement of God making his salvation known among the nations, an event he had long ago promised to their patriarchs! In the fullness of time, God had sent his Messiah to initiate this redemptive breakthrough, finally clarifying the "mystery" of the gospel (Eph 3:7-12). Those who had been far away were being brought near to God, not by adoption of a different earth culture, but by entering the kingdom of heaven through the blood of Christ. The success of this breakthrough was good news to those with right hearts attuned to the gospel. But not to everyone. The Jerusalem church missed the wonder of their age.

Little surprise, then, that the Jerusalem church never voluntarily engaged kingdom growth outside its own community. The expansion from Jerusalem into Judea and Samaria in Acts 8 was hardly an intentional sending out. It arose instead from persecution, and the apostles stayed in Jerusalem even then.

After Peter and John were eventually sent to Samaria to pray for new Samaritan believers in chapter 8, these two did indeed preach in Samaritan villages, but only on their way back to Jerusalem. If there is evidence in Acts that the Jerusalem church (other than Peter) ever engaged Gentiles at all, I can't find it.

In the cases of both Jerusalem and Antioch, the church leaders faced a demanding decision. There could be no pretense of ignorance; God had made himself clear, and their leaders had acknowledged his message.

In each case, however, choosing to live the culture of heaven would require something difficult of the church. For Antioch, it would require giving up nearly half their leadership team. For Jerusalem, it would require confronting difficult issues of ethnicity and earth culture. In each church, adoption of the culture of heaven would require courageous leadership.

In Antioch the leaders fasted and prayed before sending Paul and Barnabas out, and Antioch became the new center of God's kingdom-building activity. In Jerusalem, meanwhile, leaders repeatedly refused to confront the errant earth culture theology that was holding them back, and that church lapsed into historical irrelevance. I want to think that the Jerusalem church eventually "got it." Church tradition suggests that at least Peter and the apostles did. But the account we have in Acts, limited in time frame, presents a compelling contrast which we ignore at our churches' peril.

If you're seeing uncomfortable parallels between your church and Jerusalem, take heart. It's not too late! In the name of Jesus and in the power of God's Holy Spirit, stand up and conquer! God continues to call leaders to confront the unchallenged earth culture in our churches that hampers our full participation in what he is doing in our age. Challenging well-established but false beliefs will be costly. It will involve upsetting people. They might leave and take their money with them! But don't forget, your father owns many cows!

Refusing to remain like Jerusalem will not be enough, however. We must also choose to become like Antioch. We must identify so completely with Jesus, and live the culture of heaven so intentionally, that we become engaged in God's agenda no matter the cost.

We can only do this through him. He will show us how and make us able, like he did ancient Antioch. This isn't anything new for him. Let us strenuously seek his will together. May we hear his voice together as he calls us to pursue gospel endeavors more and more preposterous by worldly standards. May he once again gather brothers and sisters from earth culture churches unwilling to send them and put them in heaven culture churches who will. May yours be among them! Churches permeated with unchallenged earth culture may become suspicious of us, disparage us, even attack us, because they don't have heaven culture eyes. This too is part of living the culture of heaven. Jesus said so. But we will survive these attacks and grow stronger and more faithful through them.

But it won't all be grim! People we send to the advancing edge of the kingdom will come back to us with astonishingly good news, reports of God bringing spiritual light to heretofore darkened corners of the world. Our adoption of heaven culture will be affirmed and any earth culture still influencing us will be exposed. And we'll move closer and closer to the heart of God, desire his kingdom more and more, live his culture more and more, and be deceived by earth culture less and less. We will not only be looking forward to the day of God, we will be joyfully speeding its coming.

None of this will just happen by itself. Leaders, lead like men who will have to give account to God for the church under your care! Invisible influences of earth culture on it must be identified and pulled up by the roots. This will be hard.

I'll say this one more time. There will be people inside your church who won't like it. People outside your church might not like it either. Feelings may be hurt. Careers may be sacrificed. Maybe yours! But refusing to lead bravely is to accept a sidelined role for your church in God's great work. Or maybe no role at all.

9
MAKING GOD PROUD

Maybe you're feeling a bit overwhelmed with all this. Maybe you're asking yourself what God wants from you now. I can help you with that. He wants your worship. That's really what he wants, your spiritual worship. Look again at Romans 12.

> I appeal to you therefore brothers, by the mercies of God, to present your bodies as a living sacrifice, holy and acceptable to God, *which is your spiritual worship*. Do not be conformed to this world, but be transformed by the renewal of your mind, that by testing you may discern what is the will of God, what is good and acceptable and perfect.
>
> Rom 12:1-2

Living the culture of heaven is our spiritual worship song. Presenting ourselves to him without reservation is the heaven culture worship he desires. I don't know what God thinks when folks who prefer earth culture to his come to church buildings on Sunday mornings and sing songs. Maybe he enjoys the music. I don't know. I only know what scripture tells me, that God's definition of spiritual worship uses words like sacrifice and transformation. It is spiritual worship he wants, and spiritual worship is about living the culture of heaven. So worship him that way. Live the culture of heaven.

I'm sure you are familiar with Hebrews chapter 11, the "Faith Hall of Fame." The chapter recounts instances of faithfulness in the midst of extreme maltreatment, some of which are not described anywhere else in scripture. In the middle of the chapter, in verse 16, is a remarkable statement. "Therefore God is not ashamed to be called their God..." Wow! These faith heroes made God proud. He is proud to have his name associated with them!

But what about you and me? Is God proud to be called *our* God? Few of us have faced such challenges on behalf of Christ. Few of us feel like heroes. It's easy to feel like we can't measure up to them. But that isn't the point of the passage. Here's the whole verse.

> "If they had been thinking of that land
> from which they had gone out, they

would have had opportunity to return.
But as it is, they desire a better country,
a heavenly one. *Therefore* God is not
ashamed to be called their God, for he
has prepared for them a city."
                    Hebrews 11:16

Did you catch it? God wasn't proud of them because of
what they had done. He was proud of them because
they wanted heaven more than they wanted their
earthly country. God *loves* that! All the faith heroes
celebrated in Hebrews 11 had this one common trait, a
desire for heaven over anything this world could offer.
It was their overwhelming desire for heaven that fueled
their faithful deeds. *That's* why God was proud!

Brothers and sisters, *we can be like them!* We can be
driven by that same desire. If we refuse to conform to
the world and quit admiring what it offers, if we instead
allow ourselves to be overwhelmed with a simple, pure
longing for heaven, God will be just as proud of us as he
is of them.

So you've reached the end of this little book. Now go
make God proud. Quit trying to be Isaac. Look instead
to Jesus, the founder and perfecter of our faith. Desire
the better country, your heavenly home.

Let God show you how to live the culture of heaven!

10
EPILOGUE

An honest-to-goodness theologian I know read a draft of this work and suggested I include an example of a real person trying to live out the culture of heaven. He was right. I tend to focus on theory over application, but good theory doesn't effortlessly lead to good application. So here we go. I'm going to use myself as the example. Here's what one aspect of living heaven culture looks like for me, at this very moment, today.

I mentioned earlier that my wife and I have a family of Congolese asylum seekers living with us: a man, his pregnant wife, and their two sons ages four and two. They don't speak English yet, so we communicate in French. It's been three months since we took them in.

Although they're believers, their earth culture is quite different from ours. Living with us has been hard for them. Living with them has been pretty hard for us too, and it's not just the miscommunications, inconvenience, and expenses. It's the dilemmas. Here's what I mean.

They are in the U.S. legally, but our government hasn't given them work permits. These permits might take several months if they come at all. They've asked us about working illegally for cash, as do many of their asylum-seeker friends, and there are plenty of American employers who will happily oblige. But we've urged them not to do that, even though they don't like living on charity. We don't want them to break any U.S. laws and thereby jeopardize their asylum claim when they stand before an immigration judge someday. So are we putting U.S. law, which prevents them from working, above God's law, which doesn't? That's one dilemma.

When we agreed to host them, we didn't know how much it would cost us or how long it would be before they could provide for themselves. We just knew Jesus expects us to take care of strangers, so we invited them in, expecting God to work out the money some way. We also are trying to live like our Father owns everything. Our income isn't enough to support two families, but it didn't need to be. Just before they arrived, a friend gave us $1,000 "out of the blue." Folks from my group at church gave us gift cards.

Later we learned this family is eligible for public food assistance and Medicaid. Glad to have more help with expenses, we signed them up. But that presented a second dilemma. Would it have glorified God more if his people had assumed responsibility for these expenses without resorting to governmental assistance? Did we reflexively fall back to an earth culture response to our problem? We know we have brothers and sisters in Christ who would wag their fingers at the use of public funds for this family, but what we need is someone to suggest what we should do instead. Besides ignoring them.

There's more. We had enough room in our house for them until two weeks ago when my aged, memory-impaired mother came to live with us. Our house was full before, now it's beyond full. My wife and I are sleeping on the sofa while Mom sleeps in our bed. This isn't going to work long-term.

So we've found an apartment and plan to move our guests there when it's ready next month. We'll pay their rent and utilities until they can (or until we can't, whichever comes first!) but we dread telling them they must leave. Voila, a third dilemma. Who has the highest heaven culture claim to our time and our house? Am I ranking Mom's claim higher because of heaven culture or because of earth culture? But wait, there's even more still!

This is just one family. We know there are many, many other such families who need to be housed and cared for, but we can't find anyone else in our town interested in hosting a family of asylum seekers in their home. We think they exist, but we can't find them. So should we rent two apartments and bring another family up from Texas? If two, why not three? And what is the role God would have our local churches play in this, and how does he want us to help them find it?

Finally, we've been discussing asylum seekers who are here legally. But what about the strangers who *aren't* here legally? I can't read anywhere in scripture that God's expectation of us to welcome strangers only applies to strangers approved by our earthly government. He just said to welcome strangers (see Matthew 25:31-46). It's easy for me to become frustrated that our local churches don't seem to want to have anything to do with "illegal" strangers, but what about me? If it's right for churches to welcome such strangers, then it's right for me too. So why don't I?

Honestly, it's not just because of time and money. It's also because I don't want to deal with the backlash from church people. But in heaven culture, the only legitimate fear is the fear of God. How can I live heaven culture, or expect to help anyone else live it, if I fear what men may say or do to me?

So there you have it. I have trouble living heaven culture too. As I said earlier, clean theories can have messy applications. Your heaven culture application mess will likely be different from mine. God may take you on a different path, give you different gifts, and call you to a different ministry.

One thing, though, is true for all of us. God doesn't expect us to do any of this without him. We must open ourselves up to his Holy Spirit, for we need his counsel, his comfort, and his power. And we need him to continually give us that peculiar joy of being in way over our heads. That, too, is a heaven culture thing.

OK, now you've reached the end of this little book yet again. I'm praying you're better off for having read it.

Now for heaven's sake, put it down and ask God to lead you into the divine mess he has prepared for you.

And get over-your-head deep in the culture of heaven!

www.ingramcontent.com/pod-product-compliance
Lightning Source LLC
Chambersburg PA
CBHW020038040426
42331CB00030B/18